Handbook of Prayers
Student Edition

Handbook of Prayers
Student Edition

Rev. James Socias

MIDWEST THEOLOGICAL FORUM

Published in the United States of America by

MIDWEST THEOLOGICAL FORUM
4340 Cross Street, Suite 1
Downers Grove, IL 60517 USA
Tel.: (630) 541-8519
Fax: (331) 777-5819
Email: mail@mwtf.org
www.theologicalforum.org

With Ecclesiastical Approval

Published by the authority of the Bishop's Committee
on the Liturgy, National Conference of Bishops
(United States of America)

First Student Edition of *Handbook of Prayers*, excerpted from
the Seventh American Edition of *Handbook of Prayers*, 2011

ISBN 978-1-936045-00-6

To Jesus, Mary, and Joseph,
the Holy Family of Nazareth,
that from them we may learn to pray
so that our family may become
a truly Christian one.

ACKNOWLEDGMENTS

CONTENTS

Prayers After Mass

Eucharistic Adoration

Guide for a Good Confession

Devotions to the Blessed Trinity

ABBREVIATIONS FOR
THE BOOKS OF THE BIBLE

Gn	Genesis	Mi	Micah
Ex	Exodus	Na	Nahum
Lv	Leviticus	Hb	Habakkuk
Nm	Numbers	Zep	Zephaniah
Dt	Deuteronomy	Hg	Haggai
Jos	Joshua	Zec	Zechariah
Jgs	Judges	Mal	Malachi
Ru	Ruth	1 Mc	1 Maccabees
1 Sm	1 Samuel	2 Mc	2 Maccabees
2 Sm	2 Samuel		
1 Kgs	1 Kings	Mt	Matthew
2 Kgs	2 Kings	Mk	Mark
1 Chr	1 Chronicles	Lk	Luke
2 Chr	2 Chronicles	Jn	John
Ezr	Ezra	Acts	Acts
Neh	Nehemiah	Rom	Romans
Tb	Tobit	1 Cor	1 Corinthians
Jdt	Judith	2 Cor	2 Corinthians
Est	Esther	Gal	Galatians
Jb	Job	Eph	Ephesians
Ps	Psalms	Phil	Philippians
Prv	Proverbs	Col	Colossians
Eccl	Ecclesiastes	1 Thes	1 Thessalonians
Sg	Song of Songs	2 Thes	2 Thessalonians
Wis	Wisdom	1 Tm	1 Timothy
Sir	Sirach	2 Tm	2 Timothy
Is	Isaiah	Ti	Titus
Jer	Jeremiah	Phlm	Philemon
Lam	Lamentations	Heb	Hebrews
Bar	Baruch	Jas	James
Ez	Ezekiel	1 Pt	1 Peter
Dn	Daniel	2 Pt	2 Peter
Hos	Hosea	1 Jn	1 John
Jl	Joel	2 Jn	2 John
Am	Amos	3 Jn	3 John
Ob	Obadiah	Jude	Jude
Jon	Jonah	Rev	Revelation

ABBREVIATIONS

Used in This Text

CA	*Centesimus Annus* (On the Hundredth Anniversary)
CCC	*Catechism of the Catholic Church*
CIC	*Code of Canon Law* (*Codex Iuris Canonici*)
CPB	*Christ Is Passing By*, St. Josemaria Escriva (Princeton, N.J.: Scepter Publications) 1968.
CT	*Catechesi Tradendæ* (On Catechesis in our Time)
CTH	*Crossing the Threshold of Hope*, St. John Paul II (New York: Alfred A. Knopf) 1994.
DC	*Dominicæ Cœnæ* (The Lord's Supper)
DPPL	*Directory on Popular Piety and the Liturgy*
DV	*Dei Verbum* (Dogmatic Constitution on Divine Revelation)
FG	*Friends of God*, St. Josemaria Escriva (Princeton, N.J.: Scepter Publications) 1973.
FW	*Furrow*, St. Josemaria Escriva (Princeton, N.J.: Scepter Publications) 1987.
GCD	*General Catechetical Directory*
GS	*Gaudium et Spes* (Pastoral Constitution on the Church in the Modern World)
HR	*Holy Rosary*, St. Josemaria Escriva (Princeton, N.J.: Scepter Publishers) 1972.
ICEL	International Commission on English in the Liturgy
ITC	*Introduction to Catholicism* (Downers Grove, IL: Midwest Theological Forum) 2007.
LE	*Laborem Exercens* (On Human Work)
LG	*Lumen Gentium* (Dogmatic Constitution on the Church)
MC	*Marialis Cultus*

MF   *Mysterium Fidei* (The Mystery of Faith)

NLY   *General Norms for the Liturgical Year and the Calendar*

PCS   *Pastoral Care of the Sick*
       (New York: Catholic Book Publishing) 1983.

PG   J.P. Migne, ed., *Patrologia Græca* (Paris: 1857–1866)

PO   *Presbyterorum Ordinis*
       (Decree on the Ministry and Life of Priests)

RC   *Redemptoris Custos*

RCC   *The Rites of the Catholic Church*
       (New York: Pueblo Publishing Co.) 1990.

RMat   *Redemptoris Mater*, St. John Paul II, 1987.

RP   *Reconciliatio et Pænitentia*
       (On Reconciliation and Penance)

RVM   *Rosarium Virginis Mariæ*

SC   *Sacrosanctum Concilium*
       (The Constitution on the Sacred Liturgy)

SD   *Salvifici Dolores*

UTS   *Understanding the Scriptures*
       (Woodridge, IL: Midwest Theological Forum) 2008.

Way   *The Way*, St. Josemaria Escriva
       (Princeton, N.J.: Scepter Publishers) 1976.

HOW TO BE A BETTER CATHOLIC

UNIVERSAL CALL TO HOLINESS

"All Christians in any state or walk of life are called to the fullness of Christian life and to the perfection of charity."[1] "Be perfect, just as your heavenly Father is perfect."[2] God wants us to be holy and to do so one must try to sanctify oneself in one's place within the Church of Christ.

> [Lay Christians] live in the ordinary circumstances of family and social life, from which the very web of their existence is woven.[3]

> By their very vocation, they seek the Kingdom of God by engaging in temporal affairs and by ordering them according to the plan of God. They live in the world, that is, in each and in all of the secular professions and occupations.[4]

> Hence the laity, dedicated as they are to Christ and anointed by the Holy Spirit, are marvelously called and prepared so that even richer fruits of the Spirit may be produced in them. For all their works, prayers, and apostolic undertakings, family and married life, daily work, relaxation of mind and body, if they are accomplished in the Spirit—indeed even the hardships of life if patiently borne—all these become spiritual sacrifices acceptable to God through Jesus Christ. In the celebration of the Eucharist these may most fittingly be offered to the Father along with the body of the Lord. And so, worshiping everywhere by their holy actions, the laity consecrate the world itself to God, everywhere offering worship by the holiness of their lives.[5]

In order to sanctify ourselves in the ordinary circumstances of our lives, we need to grow in our spiritual lives, especially through prayer, self-denial, and work.

---

1. LG 40.
2. Mt 5: 48.
3. LG 31.
4. *Ibidem.*
5. CCC 901; cf. LG 10, 34; 1 Pt 2: 5.

Life of Prayer

"We learn to pray at certain moments by hearing the Word of the Lord and sharing in his Paschal mystery, but his Spirit is offered us at all times, in the events of *each day*, to make prayer spring up from us."[6] "Prayer in the events of each day and each moment is one of the secrets of the kingdom revealed to 'little children,' to the servants of Christ, to the poor of the Beatitudes. It is right and good to pray so that the coming of the kingdom of justice and peace may influence the march of history, but it is just as important to bring the help of prayer into humble, everyday situations; all forms of prayer can be the leaven to which the Lord compares the kingdom."[7]

> But do not imagine that prayer is an action to be carried out and then forgotten. The just man "delights in the law of the Lord and meditates on his law day and night." "Through the night, I meditate on you" and "my prayer comes to you like incense in the evening." Our whole day can be a time for prayer — from night to morning and from morning to night.[8]

Life of Self-Giving and Self-Denial

"The way of perfection passes by way of the Cross. There is no holiness without renunciation and spiritual battle. Spiritual progress entails the ascesis and mortification that gradually lead to living in the peace and joy of the Beatitudes."[9] "Without mortification there is no happiness on earth."[10]

> Let's listen to our Lord: "He who is faithful in a very little is faithful also in much; and he who is dishonest in very little is dishonest also in much." It is as if he were saying to us: "Fight continuously in the apparently unimportant things which are to my mind important; fulfill your duty punctually; smile at whoever needs cheering up, even though there is sorrow in your soul; devote the necessary time to prayer, without haggling; go to the help of anyone who looks for you; practice justice and go beyond it with the grace of charity."[11]

---

6. CCC 2659; cf. Mt 6: 11, 34.

7. CCC 2660; cf. Lk 13: 20-21.

8. CPB 119.

9. CCC 2015; cf. 2 Tm 2: 4.

10. FW 983.

11. CPB 77.

Self-denial will be more precious if it is united to charity as stated by St. Leo the Great: "Let us give to virtue what we refuse to self-indulgence. Let what we deny ourselves by fast be the refreshment of the poor."

Life of Study and Work

Human work proceeds directly from persons created in the image of God and called to prolong the work of creation by subduing the earth, both with and for one another. Hence work is a duty: "If any one will not work, let him not eat." Work honors the Creator's gifts and the talents received from him. It can also be redemptive. By enduring the hardship of work in union with Jesus, the carpenter of Nazareth and the one crucified on Calvary, man collaborates in a certain fashion with the Son of God in his redemptive work. He shows himself to be a disciple of Christ by carrying the cross, daily, in the work he is called to accomplish. Work can be a means of sanctification and a way of animating earthly realities with the Spirit of Christ.[12]

In work, the person exercises and fulfills in part the potential inscribed in his nature. The primordial value of labor stems from man himself, its author and its beneficiary. Work is for man, not man for work. Everyone should be able to draw from work the means of providing for his life and that of his family, and of serving the human community.[13]

SUMMARY OF CHRISTIAN BELIEFS

We are required to know and to believe:

- That there is one supreme, eternal, infinite God, the Creator of Heaven and earth.

- That the good will be rewarded by him forever in Heaven, and that the wicked who die unrepentant will be punished forever in Hell.

- That in the Holy Trinity there are three Persons, coeternal, coequal: God the Father, God the Son, and God the Holy Spirit.

- That the Second Person of the Holy Trinity became man and died on the Cross to save us.

---

12. CCC 2427; cf. GS 34; Gn 1: 28; 9: 14-18; CA 31; 2 Thes 3: 10; 1 Thes 4: 11; LE 27.
13. CCC 2428; cf. LE 6.

- The tenets of the *Apostles' Creed*.
- In the *Commandments of God* and the *Precepts of the Church*.
- That the *Seven Sacraments* were instituted by Christ to give us grace; especially, that Baptism is necessary and that the Eucharist is a pledge of our future glory.
- That *Sacred Tradition* and *Sacred Scripture*, which together form one sacred deposit of the Word of God, are entrusted to the Church.
- Whatever God teaches us by his Church, who in her teaching cannot deceive us or be deceived.

  The Roman Pontiff, head of the college of bishops, enjoys this infallibility in virtue of his office, when, as supreme pastor and teacher of all the faithful—who confirms his brethren in the faith—he proclaims by a definitive act a doctrine pertaining to faith or morals.... The infallibility promised to the Church is also present in the body of bishops when, together with Peter's successor, they exercise the supreme "Magisterium," above all in an Ecumenical Council. When the Church through its supreme Magisterium proposes a doctrine "for belief as being divinely revealed" and as the teaching of Christ, the definitions "must be adhered to with the obedience of faith."[14]

SPIRITUAL GAME PLAN

Love of God

Do you want to be a really good Christian? The first of your battles will be to remain in the state of grace; to avoid any mortal sin. And, then, because you want to love God above all things, you will also try not to commit venial sins.

The practice of some acts of piety throughout the day will help you to have a divine contemplative life in the midst of the daily routine. The habitual performance of these acts will also be the foundation for growing in Christian virtues. Most important is to be consistent in your daily schedule, in your spiritual game plan, so that you will live as a child of God.

---

14. CCC 891; LG 25; cf. Vatican Council I: DS 3074; DV 10§2; cf. LG 25.

Daily

- *Get up at a fixed time*, as early as possible. Eight hours of sleep should be enough. More than this or less than seven hours of sleep is usually not healthy.

- *Offer your day* to God through the intercession of our Lady (p. 35).

- *Work and study with order and intensity* during the day as a way of serving God. Set goals and establish priorities in order to develop a practical schedule. Sanctifying ordinary work is the goal of our life.

- *Attend Mass, receiving Holy Communion*, as often as possible. This is the best sacrifice we can offer to God. Prepare yourself for the Mass by spending some time in prayer.

- *Spend time in prayer* before the Blessed Sacrament (15 minutes is a good goal).

- Pray the *Angelus*. Traditionally, the *Angelus* is prayed at sunrise (6:00 A.M.), noon, and sunset (6:00 P.M.). (During Eastertime, say the *Regina Cæli* instead.)

- Pray the *Rosary* — if possible, with others — offering each decade for a specific intention.

- Do some *spiritual reading*. Start with the New Testament or some well-known spiritual book. Ten to fifteen minutes is a good goal (p. 226).

- Make a short *examination of conscience* at the end of the day before going to bed. Three minutes is enough. Follow these steps: Humble yourself in the presence of God. Tell him, "Lord, if you will, you can make me clean. "Ask for light to acknowledge your defects and virtues and to see the dangers and opportunities of the day. Ask for repentance, amendment, and encouragement (p. 40).

Weekly

- Center all activities around the *Holy Mass* on *Sunday*, the Lord's Day. It is a day for rest and spiritual growth.

- If you do not receive Holy Communion every day, receive at least on Sundays and Holy Days of Obligation. Remember to go to Confession, if needed.

- Saturday is traditionally dedicated to the Blessed Virgin Mary. Honor her and say some special prayer, such as the *Hail Holy Queen*.

Monthly

- Go to *Confession* at least once a month. God forgives our sins. The Sacrament of Penance "is the ordinary way of obtaining forgiveness and remission of mortal sins committed after Baptism." "Every serious sin must always be stated, with its determining circumstances, in an individual confession."[15]

- Seek and follow the *spiritual guidance* of a wise, prudent, and knowledgeable spiritual director.

- *Spend a few hours in a holy hour*, etc., best done before the Blessed Sacrament. Consider how you are directing your life toward God.

Yearly

- *Attend a spiritual retreat each year in silence*, speaking with God only. A few days of *retreat* are necessary for the soul in the same way that the body needs a vacation. It is a yearly opportunity for conversion.

---

15. RP 33

Always

- Stay in the *presence of God*: be aware that he is always close to you. Try to please him in everything, always remembering how much he loves you.

- *Thank God* for the graces that he constantly gives you.

- Do everything *for love of God*: this is purity of intention. Always purify your intention. Make *acts of contrition* and *atonement* for your sins and the sins of others.

- Try to *live as you would like to die*. We shall die as we have lived.

DEVOTIONS DURING THE WEEK

Sunday
: **The Blessed Trinity**
  Attend Mass and, if properly disposed, receive Communion. Cultivate in your heart a great zeal for the one and triune God.

Monday
: **The Holy Spirit**
  Pray to God the Holy Spirit to lead you to grow in holiness.

Tuesday
: **The Holy Angels**
  Pray often to your Guardian Angel asking for help.

Wednesday
: **Saint Joseph**
  Pray to St. Joseph, so that you may obtain a good and holy death.

Thursday
: **The Blessed Sacrament**
  Throughout the day, say many spiritual communions. Make a visit to the Blessed Sacrament.

Friday
: **The Passion and Death of Our Lord Jesus Christ**
  Using the Way of the Cross, meditate on the Passion and Death of our Lord.

Saturday
: **The Blessed Virgin Mary**
  Pray the Rosary or practice another Marian devotion.

THE SEVEN SACRAMENTS

The [seven] sacraments are efficacious signs of grace, instituted by Christ and entrusted to the Church, by which divine life is dispensed to us. The visible rites by which the sacraments are celebrated signify and make present the graces proper to each sacrament. They bear fruit in those who receive them with the required dispositions.[16]

Baptism[17]

By which we are born into the new life in Christ

The fruits of this Sacrament are:

- Remission of Original Sin and all personal sins.
- Birth into the new life by which we become an adoptive child of the Father, a member of Christ, and a temple of the Holy Spirit.
- Incorporation into the Church, the Body of Christ, and participation in the priesthood of Christ.
- The imprinting, on the soul, of an indelible spiritual sign, the character, which consecrates the baptized person for Christian worship. (Because of this *character*, Baptism cannot be repeated.)

Confirmation[18]

By which we are more perfectly bound to the Church and enriched with a special strength of the Holy Spirit

The fruits of this Sacrament are:

- An increase and deepening of baptismal grace.
- A deepening of one's roots in the divine filiation which makes one cry, "Abba, Father!"
- A firming of one's unity with Christ.
- An increase of the gifts of the Holy Spirit.
- A strengthening of one's bond with the Church and a closer association with her mission.

---

16. CCC 1131.
17. Cf. CCC 1279-1280.
18. Cf. CCC 1303-1304.

- A special strength of the Holy Spirit to spread and defend the faith by word and action as true witnesses of Christ, to confess the name of Christ boldly, and to never be ashamed of the Cross.
- The imprinting, as in Baptism, of a spiritual mark or indelible *character* on the Christian's soul. (Because of this *character*, one can receive this Sacrament only once in one's life.)

The Holy Eucharist[19]

*By which Christ associates his Church
and all her members with the Sacrifice offered on the Cross*

The fruits of this Sacrament are:

- An increase in the communicant's union with Christ.
- Forgiveness of venial sins.
- Preservation from grave sins.
- A strengthening of the unity of the Church as the Mystical Body of Christ, because of the strengthening of the bonds of charity between the communicant and Christ.

Reconciliation or Penance[20]

By which sins committed after Baptism are forgiven

The fruits of this Sacrament are:

- Reconciliation with God: the penitent recovers sanctifying grace.
- Reconciliation with the Church.
- Remission of the eternal punishment incurred by mortal sins.
- Remission, at least in part, of temporal punishments resulting from sin.
- Peace and serenity of conscience, and spiritual consolation.
- An increase of spiritual strength for the Christian battle.

---

19. Cf. CCC 1407, 1413–1414, 1416. "Under the consecrated species of bread and wine Christ himself, living and glorious, is present in a true, real and substantial manner: his Body and his Blood, with his soul and his divinity" (CCC 1413). The Holy Eucharist is not only a Sacrament; it is also a Sacrifice—the Holy Sacrifice of the Mass.

20. Cf. CCC 1486, 1496. "Individual and integral confession of grave sins followed by absolution remains the only ordinary means of reconciliation with God and with the Church."

Anointing of the Sick[21]

> *By which a special grace is conferred during grave illness or old age*

The fruits of this Sacrament are:

- Unity with the Passion of Christ, for the sick person's own good and that of the whole Church.
- Strength, peace, and courage to endure in a Christian manner the sufferings of illness or old age.
- Forgiveness of sins, if the sick person was not able to obtain it through the Sacrament of Penance.
- Restoration of health, if it is conducive to the salvation of the soul.
- Preparation for entering eternal life.

Holy Orders[22]

> *By which the task of serving*
> *in the name and in the person of Christ is conferred*

The fruits of this Sacrament are:

- The *mission* and *faculty* ("the sacred power") to act *in persona Christi* in three different degrees.
- Configuration to Christ as Priest, Teacher, and Pastor.
- The imprinting, as in Baptism, of an indelible *character*. (One can receive this Sacrament only once in one's life.)

Matrimony[23] (Cf. Church Laws Concerning Marriage on p. 15.)

> *By which a man and a woman form*
> *with each other an intimate communion of life and love*

The fruits of this Sacrament for the spouses are:

- The grace to love each other with the love with which Christ has loved his Church.

---

21. Cf. CCC 1527, 1532.
22. Cf. CCC 1461, 1581-1582, 1585, 1591. It is bishops who confer the Sacrament of Holy Orders in the three degrees: episcopate and presbyterate (degrees of priestly participation), and diaconate (degree of service). In the Latin Church, the Sacrament of Holy Orders for the presbyterate is normally conferred on only those candidates who are ready to embrace celibacy freely and who publicly manifest their intention of staying celibate for the love of God's kingdom and the service of others. (Cf. CCC 1576, 1579.)

- A perfecting of their human love.
- A strengthening of their indissoluble unity of the Sacrament.
- Sanctification on their way to Heaven.
- The grace to "help one another to attain holiness in their married life and in welcoming and educating their children."
- An integration into God's covenant with man: *Authentic married love is caught up into divine love.*

THE TEN COMMANDMENTS OF GOD

"Teacher, what good deed must I do, to have eternal life?"…"If you wish to enter life, keep the commandments."[24]

By his life and by his preaching Jesus attested to the permanent validity of the Decalogue…. The Decalogue contains a privileged expression of the natural law. It is made known to us by divine revelation and by human reason.[25]

1. I am the LORD your God: you shall not have strange gods before me.
2. You shall not take the name of the LORD your God in vain.
3. Remember to keep holy the LORD's Day.
4. Honor your father and your mother.
5. You shall not kill.
6. You shall not commit adultery.
7. You shall not steal.
8. You shall not bear false witness against your neighbor.
9. You shall not covet your neighbor's wife.
10. You shall not covet your neighbor's goods.

---

23. Cf. CCC 1639, 1641, 1660, 1661. The *marriage bond* has been established by God himself in such a way that a marriage concluded and consummated between baptized persons can never be dissolved.
24. Mt 19: 16–17.
25. CCC 2076, 2080.

THE PRECEPTS OF THE CHURCH[26]

The obligatory character of these positive laws decreed by the pastoral authorities is meant to guarantee to the faithful the indispensable minimum in the spirit of prayer and moral effort, in the growth in love of God and neighbor:

1. **"You shall attend Mass on Sundays and on holy days of obligation and rest from servile labor."**

   This precept requires participation in the Eucharistic celebration on the day commemorating the Resurrection of the Lord and the completion of the Sunday observance by participation in the principal liturgical feasts which honor the mysteries of the Lord, the Virgin Mary, and the saints. It also requires abstinence from those works and activities that impede the worship owed to God, the joy proper to the Lord's Day, the performance of works of mercy, or the appropriate relaxation of mind and body. Family needs or important social service can be a legitimate excuse from this obligation of rest, but the faithful should see to it that legitimate excuses do not lead to habits prejudicial to religion, family life, and health. "Never flag in zeal, be aglow with the Spirit, serve the Lord" (Rom 12: 11).

2. **"You shall confess your sins at least once a year."**

   This precept ensures preparation for the Eucharist by the reception of the Sacrament of Reconciliation, which continues Baptism's work of conversion and forgiveness. It is binding only with regard to grave sins.

3. **"You shall receive the Sacrament of the Eucharist at least during the Easter season."**

   This precept guarantees as a minimum the reception of the Lord's Body and Blood in connection with the Paschal feasts, the origin and center of the Christian liturgy.

4. **"You shall observe the days of fasting and abstinence established by the Church."**

   This precept ensures the times of abstinence and penance that prepare us for the liturgical feasts; they help us acquire freedom of heart and mastery over our instincts and freedom of heart.

5. **"You shall help to provide for the needs of the Church."**

   This precept requires the faithful to contribute to the Church according to their own abilities.

---

26. Cf. CCC 2042-2043, 2185.

HOLY DAYS OF OBLIGATION

In the United States of America

1. The Holy Days of Obligation in addition to all Sundays of the year according to the decrees[27] of the USCCB are:

   Jan 1   The Solemnity of MARY, MOTHER OF GOD

   Thursday of the Sixth Week of Easter The Solemnity of the ASCENSION

   Aug 15   The Solemnity of the ASSUMPTION OF THE BLESSED VIRGIN MARY

   Nov 1   The Solemnity of ALL SAINTS

   Dec 8   The Solemnity of the IMMACULATE CONCEPTION

   Dec 25   The Solemnity of the NATIVITY OF OUR LORD JESUS CHRIST

2. "Whenever January 1, the solemnity of Mary, Mother of God, or August 15, the solemnity of the Assumption, or November 1, the solemnity of All Saints, falls on a Saturday or on a Monday, the precept to attend Mass is abrogated."

3. The following solemnities are transferred or observed on a different day:

   Jan 6   The Solemnity of the EPIPHANY
   (shall be transferred to the first Sunday following January 1)

   Second Sunday following Pentecost The Solemnity of the MOST HOLY BODY AND BLOOD OF CHRIST
   (shall be observed on the second Sunday following Pentecost)

4. In some dioceses the celebration of the solemnity of the Ascension may be transferred. It is to be made by the affirmative vote of two-thirds of the bishops of the respective Ecclesiastical Province.

---

27. Given at the offices of the National Conference of Catholic Bishops in Washington, D.C., November 17, 1992, and August 6, 1999.

DAYS OF PENANCE

Conversion is accomplished in daily life by gestures of reconciliation, concern for the poor, the exercise and defense of justice and right, by the admission of faults to one's brethren, fraternal correction, revision of life, examination of conscience, spiritual direction, acceptance of suffering, endurance of persecution for the sake of righteousness. Taking up one's cross each day and following Jesus is the surest way of penance.[28]

Christ's faithful are obliged by divine law, each in his or her own way, to do penance. However so that all may be joined together in a common observance of penance, penitential days are prescribed in which the Christian faithful, in a special way, pray; engage in works of piety and charity; and deny themselves by fulfilling their responsibilities more faithfully, and especially by observing fast and abstinence according to the following norms:[29]

- The days and times of penance for the universal Church are the season of Lent and Fridays of the whole year. These times are particularly appropriate for spiritual exercises, penitential liturgies, pilgrimages as signs of penance, and voluntary self-denial such as fasting and almsgiving.

- Abstinence from meat (or from some other food) or another penitential practice, as determined by the conference of bishops, is to be observed on all Fridays of the year unless a solemnity should fall on a Friday. Abstinence from meat and fasting are to be observed on Ash Wednesday and on Good Friday.

- All persons who have completed their fourteenth year are bound by the law of abstinence. All adults (eighteen years or older) are bound by the law of fast up to the beginning of their sixtieth year. Pastors and parents are to see to it that even those who by reason of their age are not bound by a law of fast or abstinence are taught the true meaning of penance.

---

28. CCC 1435, 1438; cf. Am 5: 24; Isa 1: 17; cf. Lk 9: 23.
29. Cf. SC 109–110; cf. CIC 1249–1253; CCEO, cann. 880–883.

WORKS OF MERCY

The *works of mercy* are charitable actions by which we come to the aid of our neighbor's spiritual and bodily necessities. Giving alms to the poor is one of the chief witnesses to fraternal charity; it is also a work of justice pleasing to God.[30]

Corporal

- Feeding the hungry.
- Giving drink to the thirsty.
- Clothing the naked.
- Sheltering the homeless.
- Visiting the sick.
- Visiting the imprisoned.
- Burying the dead.

Spiritual

- Counseling the doubtful.
- Instructing the ignorant.
- Admonishing sinners.
- Comforting the afflicted.
- Forgiving offenses.
- Bearing wrongs patiently.
- Praying for the living and the dead.

CHURCH LAWS CONCERNING MARRIAGE[31]

Matrimony—defined as *the marriage covenant, by which a man and a woman establish between themselves a partnership of the whole of life*—is *by its nature ordered toward the good of the spouses and the procreation and education of offspring and has, between the baptized, been raised by Christ the Lord to the dignity of a Sacrament.*

Because Christ instituted this Sacrament, he also gives a man and a woman their vocation to marriage. The covenant thus involves not only a man and a woman, but also Christ. In establishing marriage as a vocation in life, God gave it the characteristics that enable human love to achieve its perfection and that allow family life to be full and fruitful. Outside marriage, or in the absence of a proper realization of its nature, the right conditions for the fruitfulness of human love and for a successful family life do not exist.

---

30. Cf. CCC 2447.
31. Socias, James. *Marriage Is Love Forever*. Princeton, N.J.: Scepter Publications, 1994, pp. 20–25; Cf. CCC 1055, 1601.

The Catholic Church has the right to establish laws regarding the validity of marriages, since marriage between the baptized is both a covenant and a Sacrament. And it is only the Catholic Church that has jurisdiction over those marriages as such, with due regard for the competence of civil authority concerning the merely civil effects. No one other than the Church has the power or authority to change ecclesiastical laws.

Unity and Indissolubility

"Unity of marriage" signifies that the *covenant* established is between one man and one woman: the husband cannot marry another woman during the lifetime of his wife, nor can the wife marry another man during the lifetime of her husband. *Polygamy* — having more than one spouse at the same time — is contrary to the equal personal dignity of men and women, who in Matrimony give themselves with a love that is total and therefore unique and exclusive.

"Indissolubility" refers to the fact that the bond of sacramental marriage cannot be broken except by the death of either the husband or the wife.

Consent

"Matrimonial consent" is an act of the will by which a man and a woman, in an irrevocable covenant, mutually give and accept each other, declaring their willingness to welcome children and to educate them. The consent must be an act of the will of each of the contracting parties, free of coercion and of serious fear arising from external circumstances. To be free means:

- *To be acting without constraint.*

- *To be unimpeded by natural or ecclesiastical law.*

Only those capable of giving valid matrimonial consent can get married: Matrimony is created through the consent of the parties — consent legitimately manifested between persons who, according to law, are capable of giving that consent.

Conditions for a Valid Marriage

1. The contracting parties must be capable, according to Church law, of giving matrimonial consent. Before Matrimony is celebrated, it must be evident that no impediment stands in the way of its valid and licit (lawful) celebration.

2. The consent given by the parties must be deliberate, fully voluntary, free, mutual, and public. Therefore, the following are incapable of contracting marriage:

   • *Persons who lack sufficient use of reason.*

   • *Persons who suffer from grave lack of discretion of judgment concerning essential matrimonial rights and duties that are to be mutually given and accepted.*

   • *Persons who, because of serious psychological illness, cannot assume the essential obligations of Matrimony.*

3. The consent must be *legitimately manifested in canonical form*, in the presence of an authorized priest or deacon and two witnesses. Canonical form does not oblige non-Catholics when they marry other non-Catholics, but only Catholics—even if only one of the two parties is Catholic—who have not left the Church by a formal act. "The priest (or deacon) who assists at the celebration of a marriage receives the consent of the spouses in the name of the Church and gives them the blessing of the Church. The presence of the Church's minister, as well as that of the witnesses, visibly expresses the fact that marriage is an ecclesial reality."

Age Requirement

As a condition for marriage, the Church requires that a man have completed his sixteenth year (one's sixteenth year is completed the day after one's sixteenth birthday) and that a woman have completed her fourteenth year of age (one's fourteenth year of age is completed the day after one's fourteenth birthday). These ages are the minima for validity. There may be civil laws, as well, regulating the minimum age for each state and country, but failure to comply with these laws does not invalidate marriage in the eyes of the Church.

Invalid Marriages

Marriage is permanent, because God established it so from the very beginning. The indissolubility of marriage is for the good of husband and wife, their children, and human society as a whole. The civil government has no power to dissolve a valid marriage — even if the marriage is between non-Catholics.

The government legislates only the civil aspects of marriage, such as ownership of property, custody of the children, etc. *Even when civil divorce is allowed by the country's law,* a valid and consummated marriage, in God's eyes, does not cease to exist until one of the parties dies. Civil divorce does not break the marriage covenant.

The Church does not have the power to dissolve a valid, sacramental marriage that has been *consummated.* She may declare a marriage *null and void* only upon investigation and on evidence that from the very beginning the marriage did not exist. Possible reasons include the following:

• Lack of fully *voluntary and free consent.*

• Some deficiency in the *form of the marriage celebration.*

• The presence of an *impediment* that makes a marriage invalid.

The *declaration of nullity* (so-called *annulment*) is a very important decision of an ecclesiastical court. A very careful investigation has to be made by the court before that conclusion can be reached, ensuring that no valid marriage is declared *null and void* by mistake.

Mixed Marriages

Marriages between two baptized persons, one of whom was baptized in the Catholic Church or received into it after Baptism and has not left it by a formal act, and the other of whom is a member of a church or ecclesial community which is not in full communion with the Catholic Church (*mixed marriages*) require *permission* (not dispensation) from the local ordinary (usually the bishop) for validity.

Marriages between two persons, one of whom was baptized in the Catholic Church or received into it after Baptism and has not left it by a formal act, and the other of whom is non-baptized (*disparity of cult* impediment) require for validity a *dispensation* from the local ordinary.

All this presupposes that these marriages are celebrated with all other necessary conditions fulfilled.

The local bishop may grant that permission or dispensation for such marriages on the following conditions (cf. CIC 1125):

- The Catholic party declares that he or she is prepared to remove dangers of falling away from the faith and makes a sincere promise to do all in his or her power to have all the children baptized and brought up in the Catholic Church.

- The other party is to be informed at an appropriate time of these promises that the Catholic person has to make. It is important that the other person be truly aware of the commitments and obligations of the Catholic spouse.

- Both persons are to be instructed with respect to the essential ends and properties of marriage, which are not to be excluded by either party.

- The man and woman should *marry in the Catholic Church*. The canonical form (Church ceremony with an authorized Catholic priest or deacon and at least two other witnesses present) is to be followed. When there are serious difficulties, the local bishop may give a dispensation and allow another form which is public (such as a civil ceremony) to be followed. It is never allowed, however, to have the Catholic priest or deacon and a non-Catholic minister, rabbi, or public official, each performing his or her own rite, asking for the consent of the parties. Likewise, it is forbidden to have another religious marriage ceremony before or after the Catholic ceremony for giving or receiving the matrimonial consent. Marriage consent is given only once.

Worthy Reception of the Sacrament of Matrimony

Once these requirements for a valid marriage are fulfilled, some other conditions are needed for the *worthy* reception of the *Sacrament* of Matrimony:

- *Baptism*. Both parties must be baptized persons.

- *Rectitude of intention*. Being carried away by emotions or momentary passions should be avoided. Premarital pregnancy is not a sufficient reason to marry someone; that could just be an added mistake.

- *Spiritual preparation*. One should be in the state of grace. The Sacraments of Penance and holy Eucharist are strongly recommended as immediate preparation.

- *Confirmation*. Catholics should have previously received the Sacrament of Confirmation. Otherwise it should be received before marriage, unless grave difficulties stand in the way.

- *Knowledge of the duties of married life*. Such duties include mutual fidelity of the spouses until death, and care for the bodily and spiritual welfare of the children sent by God.

- *Obedience to the marriage laws of the Church*.

INDULGENCES[32]

Definition

- "An indulgence is a remission before God of the temporal punishment due to sins whose guilt has already been forgiven, which the faithful Christian who is duly disposed gains under certain prescribed conditions through the action of the Church which, as the minister of redemption, dispenses and applies with authority the treasury of the satisfactions of Christ and the saints."

- "An indulgence is obtained through the Church who, by virtue of the power of binding and loosing granted her by Christ Jesus, intervenes in favor of individual Christians and opens for them the treasury of the merits of Christ and the saints to obtain from the Father of mercies the remission of the temporal punishments due for their sins. Thus the Church does not want simply to come to the aid of these Christians, but also to spur them to works of devotion, penance, and charity."

---

32. Cf. CCC 1471-1479; CIC 992-997; Paul VI, *Indulgentiarum Doctrina*, 1967, Libreria Editrice Vaticana.

Explanation

- An indulgence is partial or plenary according to its removal of either part or all of the temporal punishment due to sin. It may be applied to the living or the dead: *through indulgences the faithful can obtain — for themselves and also for the souls in purgatory — the remission of temporal punishment resulting from sin.* Because we and the faithful departed now being purified are members of the same communion of saints, one way in which we can help them is to obtain indulgences for them, so that the temporal punishments due to their sins may be remitted.

Requirements

Only one plenary indulgence may be gained on any one day. Several plenary indulgences may be gained on the basis of a single sacramental confession; only one may be gained, on the basis of a single Communion and prayer for the pope's intentions. Nevertheless another plenary indulgence could be gained at the hour of death even if that day we already have gained one.

If we are not properly disposed to receive a plenary indulgence when it is granted to us, we receive only a partial indulgence, according to the degree of perfection of our dispositions.

To gain an indulgence one must:

- Be baptized, not excommunicated, and in the state of grace at least at the time of completion of the prescribed works.
- Have at least the general intention of receiving the indulgence and fulfilling the prescribed works at the time and in the manner determined by the terms of the grant.

The *usual conditions* for gaining a plenary indulgence are, in addition to the good work to which it is attached:

- *Confession* and *Holy Communion* on the day of the performance of the good work itself, or within a few days before or after.
- *Prayer for the intentions of the pope.* For this, the recitation of one Our Father and one Hail Mary suffices, though the faithful may say any other prayer, according to their personal devotion.
- *Exclusion of all attachment to sin, even the slightest venial sin.*

As much as possible the reception of Holy Communion and prayer for the pope's intentions should take place on the same day as the prescribed work.

Plenary Indulgences

One may gain, among other ways, a *plenary indulgence* by:

- Visiting the Blessed Sacrament for half an hour.
- Reading the Bible (Sacred Scripture) for at least half an hour.
- Making the Stations of the Cross.
- Praying the Rosary (five decades) in a church or with one's family.
- Receiving the Apostolic Blessing at the hour of death.
- Visiting any parish church:
  - On the day of the titular feast of the church.
  - On August 2, the day of the "Portiuncula indulgence;" or on another suitable day to be determined by the local ordinary (usually the bishop).
  - On November 2 (this indulgence can only be applied to the dead).

  On these visits one should recite the *Our Father* and the *Creed* in addition to fulfilling the three requirements of Confession, Communion, and prayer for the pope's intentions.
- On Divine Mercy Sunday (2nd Sunday of Easter) participating in pious practices in honor of the Divine Mercy.

Partial Indulgences

A member of the faithful who, being at least inwardly contrite, performs a work carrying with it a partial indulgence receives through the Church the remission of some temporal punishment. A *partial indulgence* is, among other ways, granted to the faithful who:

- While performing of their duties and bearing the trials of life *raise their minds with humble confidence to God, adding*—even if only mentally—some pious invocation.

- In a spirit of faith and mercy *give of themselves or of their goods* to serve others in need.
- In a spirit of penance voluntarily *deprive themselves* of something which is licit for and pleasing to them.
- *Devoutly use religious articles* (crucifixes, rosaries, scapulars, medals) properly blessed by a priest or deacon.

SACRAMENTALS

Sacramentals are sacred signs which in a sense imitate the Sacraments. They signify certain effects, especially spiritual ones, which are obtained through the intercession of the Church. They prepare the faithful to receive the fruit of the Sacraments and sanctify different circumstances of life. Sacramentals may consist of *material things* or *actions*:

> Among the sacramentals blessings occupy an important place. They include both praise of God for his works and gifts, and the Church's intercession for men that they may be able to use God's gifts according to the spirit of the Gospel.[33]

Some other sacramentals are the Sign of the Cross, use of holy water, blessed rosaries, crucifixes, scapulars, and medals. *Exorcism* (expulsion of demons) is also a sacramental.

CARDINAL VIRTUES

> A virtue is a habitual and firm disposition to do good…. Four virtues play a pivotal role and accordingly are called "cardinal":[34]

- *Prudence*, which disposes the practical reason to discern, in every circumstance, one's true good and to choose the right means for achieving it.
- *Justice*, which consists in the firm and constant will to give God and neighbor their due.
- *Fortitude*, which ensures firmness in difficulties and constancy in the pursuit of the good.
- *Temperance*, which moderates the attraction of the pleasures of the senses and provides balance in the use of created goods.

---

33. CCC 1678; cf. CCC 1677.
34. CCC 1833, 1805; cf. CCC 1803, 1835–1838.

THEOLOGICAL VIRTUES

The theological virtues dispose Christians to live in a relationship with the Holy Trinity. They have God for their origin, their motive, and their object — God known by faith, God hoped in and loved for his own sake.[35]

Faith

- "Faith is the theological virtue by which we believe in God and believe all that he has said and revealed to us, and that Holy Church proposes for our belief, because he is truth itself."

- "The gift of faith remains in one who has not sinned against it. But 'faith apart from works is dead': when it is deprived of hope and love, faith does not fully unite the believer to Christ and does not make him a living member of his Body."

- "The disciple of Christ must not only keep the faith and live on it, but also profess it, confidently bear witness to it, and spread it.... Service of and witness to the faith are necessary for salvation."

Hope

- "Hope is the theological virtue by which we desire the Kingdom of Heaven and eternal life as our happiness, placing our trust in Christ's promises and relying not on our own strength, but on the help of the grace of the Holy Spirit."

- "The virtue of hope responds to the aspiration to happiness which God has placed in the heart of every man; it takes up the hopes that inspire men's activities and purifies them so as to order them to the Kingdom of Heaven; it keeps man from discouragement; it sustains him during times of abandonment; it opens up his heart in expectation of eternal beatitude. Buoyed up by hope, he is preserved from selfishness and led to the happiness that flows from charity."

- "Christian hope unfolds from the beginning of Jesus' preaching in the proclamation of the beatitudes."

---

35. CCC 1814–1818, 1820, 1822–1823, 1825–1828, 1840.

Charity

- "Charity is the theological virtue by which we love God above all things for his own sake, and our neighbor as ourselves for the love of God."

- "Jesus makes charity the *new commandment*.... 'This is my commandment, that you love one another as I have loved you.' (Jn 15: 12).... The Lord asks us to love as he does, even our *enemies*, to make ourselves the neighbor of those farthest away, and to love children and the poor as Christ himself."

- "Charity is superior to all the virtues. It is the first of the theological virtues.... The practice of all the virtues is animated and inspired by charity, which 'binds everything together in perfect harmony' (Col 3: 14)."

- "The practice of the moral life animated by charity gives to the Christian the spiritual freedom of the children of God. He no longer stands before God as a slave, in servile fear, or as a mercenary looking for wages, but as a son responding to the love of him who 'first loved us' (cf. 1 Jn 4: 19)."

GIFTS OF THE HOLY SPIRIT

The seven *gifts* of the Holy Spirit... belong in their fullness to Christ, Son of David. They complete and perfect the virtues of those who receive them. They make the faithful docile in readily obeying divine inspirations.[36]

The gifts of the Holy Spirit are:

- Wisdom
- Understanding
- Counsel
- Fortitude
- Knowledge
- Piety
- Fear of the Lord

---

36. Cf. CCC 1831; Is 11: 1-2.

FRUITS OF THE HOLY SPIRIT

The *fruits* of the Spirit are perfections that the Holy Spirit forms in us as the first fruits of eternal glory. The tradition of the Church lists twelve of them:[37]

- Charity
- Joy
- Peace
- Patience

- Kindness
- Goodness
- Generosity
- Gentleness

- Faithfulness
- Modesty
- Self-control
- Chastity

MORTAL AND VENIAL SINS

Sins are rightly evaluated according to their gravity. The distinction between mortal and venial sin, already evident in Scripture (cf. 1 Jn 5: 16–17), became part of the apostolic tradition of the Church. It is corroborated by human experience.[38]

"*Mortal sin* destroys charity in the heart" of the sinner and necessitates a new initiative of God's mercy and a conversion of heart which is normally accomplished within the setting of the sacrament of reconciliation.

"For a *sin* to be *mortal*, three conditions must together be met":

- *Grave matter* is specified by divine law (Ten Commandments) and the ultimate end of man.
- "*Full knowledge* [is] knowledge of the sinful character of the act, of its opposition to God's law."
- "*Complete consent* [is] a consent sufficiently deliberate to be a personal choice."

    Feigned ignorance and hardness of heart do not diminish, but rather increase, the voluntary character of a sin.

    Unintentional ignorance can diminish or even remove the imputability of a grave offense. But no one is deemed to be ignorant of the principles of the moral law, which are written in the conscience of every man. The promptings of feelings and passions can also diminish the voluntary and free character of the offense, as can external pressures

---

37. CCC 1832; cf. Gal 5: 22–23.
38. CCC 1854–1860, cf. CCC 1874; RP 17.

or pathological disorders. Sin committed through malice, by deliberate choice of evil, is the gravest.

One commits *venial sin* when, in a less serious matter, he does not observe the standard prescribed by the moral law, or when he disobeys the moral law in a grave matter, but without full knowledge or without complete consent.... *Venial sin* allows charity to subsist, even though it offends and wounds it.

CAPITAL SINS AND OPPOSED VIRTUES

[The capital sins] can be classified according to the virtues they oppose. They are called "capital" because they engender other sins, other vices.[39]

Capital Sins	Virtues Opposed
• Pride	• Humility
• Covetousness/Avarice	• Liberality
• Lust	• Chastity
• Anger/Wrath	• Meekness
• Gluttony	• Temperance
• Envy	• Brotherly love
• Sloth	• Diligence

THE SINS AGAINST THE HOLY SPIRIT

"Blasphemy against the Spirit will not be forgiven" (Mt 12:31). There are no limits to the mercy of God, but anyone who deliberately refuses to accept his mercy by repenting, rejects the forgiveness of his sins and the salvation offered by the Holy Spirit. Such hardness of heart can lead to final impenitence and eternal loss.[40]

Blasphemy [against the Holy Spirit] does not consist in offending the Holy Spirit in words; it consists rather in the *refusal to accept the salvation which God offers to man through the Holy Spirit, working through the power of the Cross.*

This sin blocks the person's route to Christ, and the sinner puts himself outside the range of God's forgiveness. In this sense, the sins against the Holy Spirit cannot be forgiven.

---

39. CCC 1866; cf. CCC 2540.
40. CCC 1864; cf. DV 46; Mt 12:31; cf. Mk 3:29; Lk 12:10.

SINS THAT CRY TO HEAVEN

The catechetical tradition recalls that there are "sins that cry to heaven": the blood of Abel, the sin of the Sodomites, ignoring the cry of the people oppressed in Egypt and that of the foreigner, the widow, and the orphan, injustice to the wage earner.[41]

BEATITUDES

The Beatitudes respond to the natural desire for happiness. This desire is of divine origin: God has placed it in the human heart in order to draw man to the One who alone can fulfill it…. [They] teach us the final end to which God calls us: the Kingdom, the vision of God, participation in the divine nature, eternal life, filiation, rest in God.

The Beatitudes are the heart of Jesus' preaching. They take up the promises made to the chosen people since Abraham. The Beatitudes fulfill the promises by ordering them no longer merely to the possession of a territory, but to the Kingdom of heaven:[42]

- Blessed are the poor in spirit, for theirs is the kingdom of heaven.
- Blessed are those who mourn, for they shall be comforted.
- Blessed are the meek, for they shall inherit the earth.
- Blessed are those who hunger and thirst for righteousness, for they shall be satisfied.
- Blessed are the merciful, for they shall obtain mercy.
- Blessed are the pure of heart, for they shall see God.
- Blessed are the peacemakers, for they shall be called the sons of God.
- Blessed are those who are persecuted for righteousness' sake, for theirs is the kingdom of heaven.
- Blessed are you when men revile you and persecute you and utter all kinds of evil against you falsely on my account. Rejoice and be glad, for your reward is great in heaven.

---

41. CCC 1867.
42. CCC 1716, 1718, 1726; Mt 5: 3–12.

CHRISTIAN PRAYER

Prayer is the raising of one's mind and heart to God or the requesting of good things from God.[43]

Prayer and *Christian life* are *inseparable*, for they concern the same love and the same renunciation, proceeding from love.[44]

What is prayer?

[Prayer] is commonly held to be a conversation. In a conversation there are always an "I" and a "thou" or "you." In this case the "Thou" is with a capital "T." If at first the "I" seems to be the most important element in prayer, prayer teaches that the situation is actually different. *The "Thou" is more important, because our prayer begins with God....*

In prayer, then, the true protagonist is God. The protagonist is *Christ,* who constantly frees creation from slavery to corruption and leads it toward liberty, for the glory of the children of God. The protagonist is the *Holy Spirit,* who "comes to the aid of our weakness." We begin to pray, believing that it is our own initiative that compels us to do so. Instead, we learn that it is always God's initiative within us, just as Saint Paul has written. *This initiative restores in us our true humanity; it restores in us our unique dignity.*[45]

Christian prayer tries above all to meditate on the mysteries of Christ: to get to know him, love him, and be united to him. We learn what prayer is by reviewing the life of Christ. He taught us how to pray. When Jesus prayed to his Father, he was already teaching us how to pray.[46]

The Church invites the faithful to regular prayer: daily prayers, the Liturgy of the Hours, Sunday Eucharist, the feasts of the liturgical year.[47]

---

43. CCC 2559; St. John Damascene, *De fide orth.* 3, 24; in PG 94, 1089C.
44. CCC 2745.
45. CTH 16-17.
46. Cf. CCC 2607, 2708.
47. CCC 2720.

Types of Prayer

Prayer in the events of each day and each moment is one of the secrets of the kingdom revealed to "little children," to the servants of Christ, to the poor of the Beatitudes. It is right and good to pray so that the coming of the kingdom of justice and peace may influence the march of history, but it is just as important to bring the help of prayer into humble, everyday situations; all forms of prayer can be the leaven to which the Lord compares the kingdom.[48]

The Christian tradition comprises three major expressions of the life of prayer:[49]

- *Vocal prayer*, founded on the union of body and soul in human nature, associates the body with the interior prayer of the heart, following Christ's example of praying to his Father and teaching the Our Father to his disciples.

- *Meditation* is a prayerful quest engaging thought, imagination, emotion, and desire. Its goal is to make our own in faith the subject considered, by confronting it with the reality of our own life.

- *Contemplative prayer* is the simple expression of the mystery of prayer. It is a gaze of faith fixed on Jesus, an attentiveness to the Word of God, a silent love. It achieves real union with the prayer of Christ to the extent that it makes us share in his mystery.

---

48. CCC 2660; cf. Lk 13: 20–21.
49. Cf. CCC 2721-2724.

The Battle of Prayer

> Prayer presupposes an effort, or fight against ourselves and the wiles of the Tempter. The battle of prayer is inseparable from the necessary "spiritual battle" to act habitually according to the Spirit of Christ: we pray as we live, because we live as we pray.[50]

The principal difficulties that we find are:

- "We don't have the time." Prayer is considered as an occupation incompatible with all the other things we have to do.

  The *remedy*: Make the time for your personal prayer, knowing that nothing could excuse your failing to do so.

- "We get distracted." Concentration becomes difficult and we easily give up.

  The *remedy*: Turn your heart back to God, offering him the distractions with humility, without discouragement.

- "We feel dry." It seems that the heart is separated from God, with no taste for thoughts, memories, and feelings, even spiritual ones.

  The *remedy*: Remember that "unless the grain of wheat falls into the earth and dies, it remains alone; but if it dies, it bears much fruit."

There are also two frequent temptations that threaten prayer:

- Lack of faith. Prayer is not the first priority.

  The *remedy*: Ask our Lord with a humble heart, "Lord, increase my faith."

- Acedia, a form of depression stemming from lax ascetical practice that leads to discouragement.

  The *remedy*: Trust God more and hold fast in constancy.

---

50. Cf. CCC 2752; 2754-2755.

THE CALL TO HOLINESS[51]

"The man who approaches the Church with misgivings sees only the closed doors, the barriers, and the windows where you buy a ticket, a kind of spiritual police station.

"But our Church is the Church of the saints.

"To become a saint, what bishop would not give his mitre, his ring, and his pectoral cross; what cardinal would not sacrifice his [red] and what pontiff his white robe, his chamberlains, his Swiss guard and all his temporal appurtenance. Who would not crave the strength to brave this marvelous adventure? For sanctity is an adventure; it is even the only adventure.

"Once you have understood this, you have entered into the heart of the Catholic faith; your mortal flesh will have trembled, no longer with a fear of death, but with a superhuman hope....

"God did not create the Church to ensure the prosperity of the saints, but in order to transmit their memory.... They lived and suffered as we do. They were tempted as we are. The man who dares not yet accept what is sacred and divine in their example will at least learn from it the lesson of heroism and honor....

"None of us will ever know enough theology to become a priest. But we know enough to be a saint. . . .Ever since God, himself, came to visit us, is there anything saints have not taken upon themselves? Is there anything which is beyond their capacity to give?"

—*Georges Bernanos*

---

51. ITC 2.

BASIC PRAYERS

A certain memorization of the words of Jesus, of important Bible passages... of some essential prayers... far from opposing the dignity of young Christians, or constituting an obstacle to personal dialogue with the Lord, is a real need.... What is essential is that the text that are memorized must at the same time be taken in and gradually understood in depth, in order to become a source of Christian life on the personal level and the community level.[1]

THE SIGN OF THE CROSS (SIGNUM CRUCIS)

We should begin our day and our activities with the Sign of the Cross. The Sign of the Cross strengthens us in temptations and difficulties.

In nómine Patris, et Fílii, et Spíritus Sancti. Amen.	In the name of the Father, and of the Son, and of the Holy Spirit. Amen.
Per signum crucis de inimícis nostris líbera nos, Deus noster. In nómine Patris...	By the sign of the cross deliver us from our enemies, you who are our God. In the name...

THE LORD'S PRAYER (PATER NOSTER)

In the Our Father, the object of the first three petitions is the glory of the Father: the sanctification of his name, the coming of the kingdom, and the fulfillment of his will. The four others present our wants to him: they ask that our lives be nourished, healed of sin, and made victorious in the struggle of good over evil.... By the final "Amen," we express our *"fiat"* concerning the seven petitions: "So be it."[2]

---

1. CT 55.
2. CCC 2857, 2865.

Pater noster, qui es in cælis: sanctificétur nomen tuum; advéniat regnum tuum; fiat volúntas tua, sicut in cælo, et in terra.

Our Father, who art in heaven, hallowed be thy name. Thy kingdom come; thy will be done on earth as it is in heaven.

Panem nostrum cotidiánum da nobis hódie; et dimítte nobis débita nostra, sicut et nos dimíttimus debitóribus nostris; et ne nos indúcas in tentatiónem; sed líbera nos a malo. Amen.

Give us this day our daily bread; and forgive us our trespasses as we forgive those who trespass against us; and lead us not into temptation, but deliver us from evil. Amen.

THE HAIL MARY (AVE MARIA)

The greeting of the angel Gabriel opens this prayer. It is God himself who, through his angel as intermediary, greets Mary.... The grace with which Mary is filled is the presence of him who is the source of all grace.... Because she gives us Jesus, her son, Mary is Mother of God and our mother; we can entrust all our cares and petitions to her. She prays for us as she prayed for herself: "Let it be to me according to your word" (Lk 1: 38). By entrusting ourselves to her prayer, we abandon ourselves to the will of God together with her..... And our trust broadens further to surrender "the hour of our death" wholly to her care. May she be there as she was at her son's death on the cross. May she welcome us as our mother at the hour of our passing to lead us to her son, Jesus, in paradise.[3]

Ave, María, grátia plena, Dóminus tecum; benedícta tu in muliéribus, et benedíctus fructus ventris tui, Iesus.

Hail, Mary, full of grace, the Lord is with thee; blessed art thou among women, and blessed is the fruit of thy womb, Jesus.

Sancta María, Mater Dei, ora pro nobis peccatóribus, nunc et in hora mortis nostræ. Amen.

Holy Mary, Mother of God, pray for us sinners, now and at the hour of our death. Amen.

---

3. CCC 2676-2677; Lk 1: 38; cf. Jn 19: 27.

THE GLORY BE / THE DOXOLOGY (GLORIA PATRI)

The Glory Be, perhaps derived from Christ's command to the Apostles to baptize "in the name of the Father, and of the Son, and of the Holy Spirit" (Mt 28: 19) has been prayed since the first centuries of Christianity.

This hymn of praise to the triune God joins us with the heavenly hosts in glorifying God. With the Glory Be we also profess, in a formula against the heresies of Arius (who denied the divinity of the Son) and of Macedonius (who denied the divinity of the Holy Spirit), our faith in the most fundamental and basic mystery of Revelation: the mystery of the Holy Trinity.

Glória Patri, et Fílio, et Spirítui Sancto.	Glory be to the Father, and to the Son, and to the Holy Spirit.
Sicut erat in princípio et nunc et semper et in sǽcula sæculórum. Amen.	As it was in the beginning, is now, and ever shall be, world without end. Amen.

MORNING OFFERING

O Jesus, through the Immaculate Heart of Mary, I offer you my prayers, works, joys, and sufferings of this day for all the intentions of your Sacred Heart, in union with the holy sacrifice of the Mass throughout the world, in thanksgiving for your favors, in reparation for my sins, for the intentions of all my relatives and friends, and in particular for the intentions of the Holy Father. Amen.

CONSECRATION TO THE BLESSED VIRGIN MARY

My Queen and my Mother, I give myself entirely to you, and, in proof of my affection, I give you my eyes, my ears, my tongue, my heart, my whole being without reserve. Since I am your own, keep me and guard me as your property and possession. Amen.

PRAYER FOR THE POPE

℣. Let us pray for our Sovereign Pontiff N.

℟. **The Lord preserve him and give him life, and make him blessed upon the earth, and deliver him not to the will of his enemies.**

ACT OF FAITH

O my God, I firmly believe that you are one God in three divine Persons, Father, Son, and Holy Spirit. I believe that your divine Son became man and died for our sins, and that he shall come to judge the living and the dead. I believe these and all the truths that the holy Catholic Church teaches, because you have revealed them, who can neither deceive nor be deceived.

ACT OF HOPE

O my God, relying on your almighty power and infinite mercy and promises, I hope to obtain pardon for my sins, the help of your grace, and life everlasting, through the merits of Jesus Christ, my Lord and Redeemer.

ACT OF CHARITY

O my God, I love you above all things, with my whole heart and soul, because you are all-good and worthy of all my love. I love my neighbor as myself for the love of you. I forgive all who have injured me and ask pardon of all whom I have injured.

PRAYER BEFORE A DAY'S WORK

Direct, we beg you, O Lord, our actions by your holy inspirations, and grant that we may carry them out with your gracious assistance, that every prayer and work of ours may begin always with you, and through you be happily ended. Amen.

ABANDONMENT TO GOD'S PROVIDENCE[5]

My Lord and my God: into your hands I abandon the past and the present and the future, what is small and what is great, what amounts to a little and what amounts to a lot, things temporal and things eternal. Amen.

---

5. *Way*, 7th station, point for meditation #3.

PRAYER TO KEEP THE PRESENCE OF GOD

Lord, God Almighty, you have brought us safely to the beginning of this day. Defend us today by your mighty power, so that we may not fall into any sin, and that all our words may so proceed and all our thoughts and actions be so directed as to be always just in your sight. Through Christ our Lord. Amen.

PRAYER TO ONE'S GUARDIAN ANGEL

Angel of God, my guardian dear, to whom God's love commits me here, ever this day (night) be at my side, to light and guard, to rule and guide. Amen

APOSTLES' CREED

The Apostles' Creed is rightly considered to be a faithful summary of the Apostles' faith. It is the ancient baptismal symbol of the Church of Rome.[4]

I believe in God,
the Father almighty,
Creator of heaven and earth,
and in Jesus Christ, his only Son, our Lord,

At the words that follow, up to and including, the Virgin Mary, all bow:
Who was conceived by the Holy Spirit,
born of the Virgin Mary,
suffered under Pontius Pilate,
was crucified, died and was buried;
he descended into hell;
on the third day he rose again from the dead;
he ascended into heaven,
and is seated at the right hand of God the Father almighty;
from there he will come to judge the living and the dead.

I believe in the Holy Spirit, /the holy catholic Church,
the communion of saints, /the forgiveness of sins,
the resurrection of the body, /and life everlasting. Amen.

ANGELUS

(outside Easter Time)

℣. Angelus Dómini nuntiávit Maríæ.

℣. The angel of the Lord declared unto Mary;

℟. **Et concépit de Spíritu Sancto.**

℟. **And she conceived by the Holy Spirit.**

Ave María.

Hail Mary.

℣. Ecce ancílla Dómini.

℣. Behold the handmaid of the Lord.

℟. **Fiat mihi secúndum verbum tuum.**

℟. **Be it done unto me according to your word.**

Ave María.

Hail Mary.

℣. Et Verbum caro factum est,

℣. And the Word was made flesh,

℟. **Et habitávit in nobis.**

℟. **And dwelt among us.**

Ave María.

Hail Mary.

℣. Ora pro nobis, sancta Dei Génetrix.

℣. Pray for us, O holy Mother of God,

℟. **Ut digni efficiámur promissiónibus Christi.**

℟. **That we may be made worthy of the promises of Christ.**

Orémus.

Let us pray.

Grátiam tuam, quæsumus, Dómine, méntibus nostris infúnde; ut qui, ángelo nuntiánte, Christi Fílii tui incarnatiónem cognóvimus, per passiónem eius et crucem, ad resurrectiónis glóriam perducámur. Per eúmdem Christum Dóminum nostrum.

Pour forth, we beseech you, O Lord, your grace into our hearts, that we, to whom the incarnation of Christ, your Son, was made known by the message of an angel, may by his passion and cross be brought to the glory of his resurrection, through the same Christ our Lord.

℟. **Amen.**

℟. **Amen.**

REGINA CÆLI
(for Easter Time) Attributed to Gregory V (+998)

℣. Regína cæli, lætáre. Allelúia.

℟. **Quia quem meruísti portáre. Allelúia.**

℣. Resurréxit, sicut dixit. Allelúia.

℟. **Ora pro nobis Deum. Allelúia.**

℣. Gaude et lætáre, Virgo María. Allelúia.

℟. **Quia surréxit Dóminus vere. Allelúia.**

Orémus.

Deus, qui per resurrectiónem Fílii tui, Dómini nostri Iesu Christi mundum lætificáre dignátus es: præsta, quæsumus;, ut, per eius Genetrícem Vírginem Maríam, perpétuæ capiámus gáudia vitæ. Per eúmdem Christum Dóminum nostrum.

℟. **Amen.**

℣. Queen of heaven, rejoice! Alleluia.

℟. **For he whom you did merit to bear. Alleluia.**

℣. Has risen, as he said. Alleluia.

℟. **Pray for us to God. Alleluia.**

℣. Rejoice and be glad, O Virgin Mary. Alleluia.

℟. **For the Lord is truly risen. Alleluia.**

Let us pray.

O God, who gave joy to the world through the resurrection of your Son our Lord Jesus Christ, grant, we beseech you, that through the intercession of the Virgin Mary, his Mother, we may obtain the joys of everlasting life, through the same Christ our Lord.

℟. **Amen.**

BRIEF EXAMINATION AT NIGHT

Make a brief examination of conscience before going to bed at night. Two or three minutes will suffice.

- **Place yourself in the presence of God**, recognizing his strength and your weakness. Tell him: "Lord, if you will, you can make me clean."

- **Ask your guardian angel for light** to acknowledge your defects and virtues: *What have I done wrong? What have I done right? What could I have done better?*

- **Examine your conscience** with sincerity:

  Did I often consider that God is my Father? Did I offer him my work? Did I make good use of my time? Did I pray slowly and with attention? Did I try to make life pleasant for other people? Did I criticize anyone? Was I forgiving? Did I pray and offer some sacrifices for the Church, for the Pope, and for those around me? Did I allow myself to be carried away by sensuality? By pride?

- **Make an act of contrition**, sorrowfully asking our Lord's pardon.

- **Make a specific resolution** for tomorrow:
  —*To stay away from certain temptations.*
  —*To avoid some specific faults.*
  —*To exert special effort to practice some virtue.*
  —*To take advantage of occasions for improvement.*

- **Pray three Hail Marys** to the Virgin Mary, asking for purity of heart and body.

I CONFESS

I confess to almighty God
and to you, my brothers and sisters,
that I have greatly sinned
in my thoughts and in my words,
in what I have done and in what I have failed to do,
through my fault, through my fault,
through my most grievous fault;
therefore I ask blessed Mary ever-Virgin,
all the Angels and Saints,
and you, my brothers and sisters,
to pray for me to the Lord our God.

ACT OF CONTRITION

O my God, I am heartily sorry for having offended you, and I detest
all my sins, because I dread the loss of heaven and the pains of hell;
but most of all because they offend you, my God, who are all good
and deserving of all my love. I firmly resolve, with the help of your
grace, to confess my sins, to do penance, and to amend my life.
Amen.

PRAYER FOR VOCATIONS

Lord Jesus Christ, shepherd of souls, who called the apostles to be
fishers of men, raise up new apostles in your holy Church. Teach
them that to serve you is to reign: to possess you is to possess all
things. Kindle in the hearts of our young people the fire of zeal for
souls. Make them eager to spread your Kingdom upon earth. Grant
them courage to follow you, who are the Way, the Truth, and the
Life; who live and reign for ever and ever. Amen.

ACCEPTANCE OF DEATH

O Lord, my God, from this moment on I accept with a good will, as something coming from your hand, whatever kind of death you want to send me, with all its anguish, pain, and sorrow.

JESUS, MARY, AND JOSEPH

℣. Jesus, Mary, and Joseph,

℟. **I give you my heart and my soul.**

℣. Jesus, Mary, and Joseph,

℟. **Assist me in my last agony.**

℣. Jesus, Mary, and Joseph,

℟. **May I sleep and take my rest
in peace with you.**

PREPARATION FOR MASS

INTRODUCTION

When our Lord instituted the Eucharist during the last supper, night had already fallen. This indicated, according to St. John Chrysostom, that 'the times had run their course.' The world had fallen into darkness, for the old rites, the old signs of God's infinite mercy to mankind, were going to be brought to fulfillment. The way was opening to a new dawn—the new passover. The Eucharist was instituted during that night, preparing in advance for the morning of the resurrection.

We too have to prepare for this new dawn. Everything harmful, worn out, or useless has to be thrown away—discouragement, suspicion, sadness, cowardice. The Holy Eucharist gives the sons of God a divine newness and we must respond in 'the newness of your mind,' renewing all our feelings and actions. We have been given a new principle of energy, strong new roots grafted onto our Lord. We must not return to the old leaven, for we have the bread which lasts for ever.[1]

Think of the human experience of two people who love each other and yet are forced to part. They would like to stay together forever, but duty—in one form or another—forces them to separate. They are unable to fulfill their desire of remaining close to each other, so man's love—which, great as it may be, is limited—seeks a symbolic gesture. People who make their farewells exchange gifts or perhaps a photograph with a dedication so ardent that it seems almost enough to burn that piece of paper. They can do no more, because a creature's power is not great as its desire.

What we cannot do, our Lord is able to do. Jesus Christ, perfect God and perfect man, leaves us, not a symbol, but a reality. He himself stays with us. He will go to the Father, but he will also remain among men. He will leave us not simply a gift that will make us remember him, not an image that becomes blurred with time, like a photograph that soon fades and yellows, and has no meaning except for those who were contemporaries. Under the appearances of bread and wine,

---

1. CPB 155.
2. CPB 83.

he is really present, with his body and blood, with his soul and divinity.[2]

Our Lord said: "I tell you most solemnly, if you do not eat the flesh of the Son of Man and drink his blood, you will not have life in you" (Jn 6: 53).

> Communion with the Body and Blood of Christ increases the communicant's union with the Lord, forgives his venial sins, and preserves him from grave sins. Since receiving this sacrament strengthens the bonds of charity between the communicant and Christ, it also reinforces the unity of the Church as the Mystical Body of Christ. The Church warmly recommends that the faithful receive Holy Communion each time they participate in the celebration of the Eucharist; she obliges them to do so at least once a year.[3]

In order to receive Holy Communion worthily, we must first confess any mortal sin we may remember. Venial sins are forgiven with a fervent Communion, works of mercy, acts of sorrow, etc.

> Anyone who desires to receive Christ in eucharistic communion must be in the state of grace. Anyone aware of having sinned mortally must not receive Communion without having received absolution in the sacrament of Penance.[4]

> Sometimes, indeed quite frequently, everybody participating in the eucharistic assembly goes to Communion; and on some such occasions, as experienced pastors confirm, there has not been due care to approach the sacrament of Penance so as to purify one's conscience. This can of course mean that those approaching the Lord's table find nothing on their conscience, according to the objective law of God, to keep them from this sublime and joyful act of being sacramentally united with Christ. But there can also be, at least at times, another idea behind this: the idea of the Mass as only a banquet in which one shares by *receiving the body of Christ in order to manifest, above all else, fraternal communion*. It is not hard to add to these reasons a certain human respect and mere *conformity*.

> This phenomenon demands from us watchful attention and a theological and pastoral analysis guided by a sense of great responsibility. We cannot allow the life of our communities to lose the good quality of sensitiveness of Christian conscience, guided solely by respect for Christ, who, when he is received in the Eucharist, should find in the heart of each of us a worthy abode. This question is closely

---

3. CCC 1416-1417.
4. CCC 1415.

linked not only with the practice of the sacrament of Penance but also with a correct sense of responsibility for the whole deposit of moral teaching and for the precise distinction between good and evil, a distinction which then becomes for each person sharing in the Eucharist the basis for a correct judgment of self to be made in the depths of the personal conscience. St. Paul's words, 'Let a man examine himself,' are well known; this judgment is an indispensable condition for a personal decision whether to approach Eucharistic Communion or to abstain.[5]

We must fast one hour before Communion. Water and medicines do not break the fast. The elderly and those who are sick, as well as those caring for them, may receive Holy Communion even if they have consumed something within the preceding hour. (cf. CIC 919).

One should receive Holy Communion with utmost reverence and devotion, bearing in mind that Christ himself, and not just an ordinary piece of bread, is being received. In some countries where the Holy See has confirmed the deliberation of the Bishops' Conference, Holy Communion may be taken in the hand. Every communicant, however, always has the right to receive Holy Communion on the tongue.

INTERNAL PREPARATION

To celebrate and/or to offer the Holy Mass with greater fruit, we may consider that:

- The Eucharistic sacrifice is the most important event that happens each day. The Eucharistic sacrifice is the center of Christian life. All the other Sacraments, and all our prayers, visits to the Blessed Sacrament, devotions, mortifications offered to God, and apostolic activities as well, have the Mass as their central point of reference. If the center were to disappear and attendance at Mass were to be consciously abandoned, then the whole Christian life would collapse.

- The Eucharistic sacrifice is the most pleasing reality we can offer to God. Every member of the Mystical Body of Christ receives at Baptism the right and duty of taking part in the sacrifice of the Head of that Body. Our Mother the Church wants us to take part in the Mass, not as strangers or passive spectators, but with an effort

---

5. DC 11.

to understand it better each time. We are to participate in the Mass in a conscious, pious, and active manner, with right dispositions and cooperating with divine grace.

- It is a good habit to pray on the way to Mass. Whether you drive or walk, turn your attention to the coming celebration. Pray for the priest, that he will minister to the needs of the parish. Pray for the congregation, that they will open their minds and hearts to what is being taught at the Mass.

- We offer this sublime sacrifice in union with the Church. Live the Holy Mass feeling part of the Church, the Mystical Body of Christ, the people of God. Be united to the bishop of the diocese where the Mass is being offered and to the Pope, the vicar of Christ for the universal Church.

- We must be united to the Sacrifice of Jesus, who is the only victim. Through him, we also offer to God the Father with the Holy Spirit all the sacrifices, sufferings, self-denials, and tribulations of each day.

- To receive Holy Communion, we need not only to be in the state of grace but to have the right intention and keep the Eucharistic fast.

You can now pray the Offering to the Merciful Love:

- Holy Father,
  through the Immaculate Heart of Mary
  I offer you Jesus, your dearly beloved Son,
  and I offer myself through him, with him, and in him,
  for all his intentions
  and in the name of all creatures.

As immediate preparation, excite in your soul lively sentiments of faith, humility, and desire. Ask yourself:

—*Who becomes present?*

—*To whom does he become present?*

—*Why does he become present?*

PRAYER OF ST. AMBROSE

I draw near to the table of your most delectable banquet, dear Lord Jesus Christ. A sinner, I trust not in my own merit; but, in fear and trembling, I rely on your mercy and goodness. I have a heart and a body marked by many grave offenses, and a mind and tongue that I have not guarded well. For this reason, God of loving kindness and awesome majesty, I, a sinner caught by many snares, seek safe refuge in you. For you are the fountain of mercy. I would fear to draw near to you as my judge, but I seek you out as my Savior.

Lord, I show you my wounds, and I let you see my shame. Knowing my sins are many and great, I have reason to fear. But I trust in your mercies, for they are beyond all numbering.

Look upon me with mercy, for I trust in you, my Lord Jesus Christ, eternal king, God and man, you who were crucified for mankind.

Have mercy on me, you who never cease to make the fountain of your mercy flow, for I am full of sorrows and sins. I praise you, the saving Victim offered on the wood of the cross for me and for all mankind. I praise the noble Blood that flows from the wounds of my Lord Jesus Christ, the precious Blood that washes away the sins of all the world.

Remember, Lord, your creature, whom you have redeemed with your own Blood. I am sorry that I have sinned, and I long to put right what I have done. Most kind Father, take away all my offenses and sins, so that, purified in body and soul, I may be made worthy to taste the Holy of holies. And grant that this holy meal of your Body and Blood, which I intend to take, although I am unworthy, may bring forgiveness of my sins and wash away my guilt. May it mean the end of my evil thoughts and the rebirth of my better longings. May it lead me securely to live in ways that please you, and may it be a strong protection for body and soul against the plots of my enemies. Amen.

PRAYER OF ST. THOMAS AQUINAS

Almighty and ever-living God, I draw near to the sacrament of your only-begotten Son, our Lord Jesus Christ. I come sick to the physician of life, unclean to the fountain of mercy, blind to the light of eternal brightness, poor and needy to the Lord of heaven and earth. So I ask you, most generous Lord: graciously heal my infirmity, wash me clean, illumine my blindness, enrich my poverty, and clothe my nakedness. May I receive the Bread of angels, the King of kings and Lord of lords, with such reverence and humility, such contrition and devotion, such purity and faith, and such resolve and determination as may secure my soul's salvation. Grant as I may receive not only the visible sign of the Lord's Body and Blood, but also all the reality and the power of the sacrament. Grant, most kind God, that I may receive the Body of your only-begotten Son, our Lord Jesus Christ, which he received from the Virgin Mary, and may receive it in such a way that I become a living part of his Mystical Body and counted among his members.

O most loving Father, grant me your beloved Son. While on this earthly pilgrimage, I receive him under the veil of this sacrament; so may I come at last to see him face to face for all eternity. For he lives and reigns with you for ever and ever. Amen.

THE EUCHARISTIC SACRIFICE

This Is the Mass

The Mass, the memorial of the Death and Resurrection of the Lord—in which the sacrifice of the Cross is perpetuated over the centuries—is the summit and source of all Christian worship and life; it signifies and effects the unity of the people of God and achieves the building up of the body of Christ. It is an action of Christ himself and the Church; in it Christ the Lord, by the ministry of a priest, offers himself, substantially present under the forms of bread and wine, to God the Father and gives himself as spiritual food to the faithful who are associated with his offering.[1]

The Mass: Christ on the Cross

We are born to live. Christ, however, was born to die. On the night of the Last Supper, Christ instituted the Mass in order to leave a memorial to his beloved Spouse, the Church. He offered his Body and Blood under the species of bread and wine to God the Father.

Taking bread, Christ said: "This is my body, which will be given up for you." Also taking the chalice with wine, he said: "This is the cup of my blood, the blood of the new and everlasting covenant. It will be shed for you and for all so that sins may be forgiven." Christ then commanded his Apostles: "Do this in memory of me," making them priests of the New Testament. This rite anticipated the bloody sacrifice that Christ accomplished on the Cross once and for all on Good Friday for the redemption of the world.

The Church continues to offer the sacrifice of the Cross, but in a bloodless manner. The Mass is neither a repetition of nor a substitute for the Cross, but the merit we gain from the Mass is the same merit that we would have gained had we actually been present at the foot of the Cross on Calvary.

---

1. Cf. *Codex Iuris Canonici* (=CIC) 897, 899.

The historical event of Calvary does not, however, repeat itself, nor is it continued in each Mass. The sacrifice of Christ is perfect and, therefore, does not need to be repeated. Glorious in Heaven, Christ does not die again. His sacrifice is not repeated; rather, the presence of the singular sacrifice of the Cross is multiplied, overcoming time and space.

The Mass: The Sacrifice of the New Covenant

Of the Sacrifice of Christ, the main sign or figure of the Sacrifice of Christ in the Old Testament is the paschal lamb. At every Passover, the Jews recalled and renewed their covenant with God by sacrificing a lamb. This sacrificial lamb once spared the firstborn of the Jews from the exterminating angel who came to slay the firstborn of every family in Egypt.

Our Lord anticipates his sacrifice on the Cross in the Last Supper, within the Jewish ritual celebration of the Passover. In the Cenacle as on Calvary, the essential elements of the Sacrifice are there: the immolation and self-offering (Body and Blood) to God the Father. Christ is the unspotted Lamb. He sets all people free from the slavery of sin and establishes the eternal alliance between creature and Creator, the New Covenant. More than that, what had been only a foreshadowing in sign is now fully realized: the communion of blood and of life between God and us.

When the faithful are said to offer Mass together with the priest, this does not mean that all the members of the Church, like the priest himself, perform the visible liturgical rite. This is done by the celebrant only. He has been divinely appointed for this purpose through the Sacrament of Holy Orders. The principal victim of the sacrifice, is Jesus Christ. But the faithful, in order to exercise their common priesthood fully, should unite their sacrifice to his and thus offer themselves, also, to God the Father: "I exhort you... to present your bodies as a living sacrifice, holy, pleasing to God—your spiritual service," wrote St. Paul to the Romans.[2]

> [The Mass] requires all Christians, so far as human power allows, to reproduce in themselves the sentiments that Christ had when he was offering himself in sacrifice: sentiments of humility, adoration, praise and thanksgiving to the divine Majesty. It requires them also to become victims, as it were, cultivating a spirit of self-denial

2. Romans 12: 1.

according to the precepts of the Gospel, willingly doing works of penance, detesting and expiating their sins. It requires us all, in a word, to die mystically with Jesus Christ on the cross, so that we may say with the same apostle: "With Christ, I hang upon the cross."[3]

The Mass: The Sacrifice of the Church

Christ bequeathed his sacrifice to the Church, not just to each individual believer. God wants to save us, not in an isolated manner, prescinding from any relationship among them, but as a people. Each Mass presupposes union among the faithful and of the faithful with their bishop, the Pope, and the universal Church. Moreover, that solid union is made stronger with the celebration of the Eucharist and is a consequence of it. The Second Vatican Council states it in this manner: "In the sacrament of the eucharistic bread, the unity of believers, who form one body in Christ,[4] is both expressed and brought about."[5]

Both on the Cross and in the Mass, the priest and victim are one and the same: Christ himself. He is both the one who offers and the one who is offered. No longer is there separation between priests and victims.

The words of Jesus Christ at the Last Supper—"Do this in memory of me"—command the continuation of his sacrifice on the Cross in every Holy Mass celebrated anywhere in the world until the end of time. This was announced in the Old Testament with these words of the prophet Malachi: "From the rising of the sun to its setting my name is great among the nations, and in every place there is a sacrifice and there is offered to my name a clean oblation."[6]

Following Christ's command, the priest offers the Mass acting as the representative of Christ. That is why he does not say, "This is the body and blood of Christ," but rather, "This is my body" and "This is my blood." The priest is the chosen instrument of Christ in the same manner that the brush is the painter's tool.

In the Mass, Christ is no longer alone on the Cross. As in any other sacrament, the Mass is an action of Christ and also of the Church. At

---

3. Pius XII, *Mediator Dei*, November 20, 1942, no. 78.

4. Cf. 1 Cor 10: 17.

5. Vatican Council II, *Lumen Gentium* (=LG) 3.

6. Malachi 1:11.

the moment of the preparation of the gifts the entire Church presents itself for sacrifice with Christ.

We have testimonies from the very beginning of the life of the Church that the Christians had the celebration of the Holy Mass on Sunday, the Lord's Day, when the victory and triumph of the Lord's death became present.

In the Old Testament, the Jews rested on Saturday, giving thanks to God for the gift of creation. In the New Testament, we celebrate a new creation, to the life of grace: a supernatural creation far superior to the material creation of the world. No wonder, then, that the Church requires under pain of mortal sin that we to go to Mass at least on Sunday.

> The holy Mass cheers the heavenly court; it alleviates the poor souls in purgatory; it attracts all sorts of blessings to the earth; it gives more glory to God than all the sufferings of the martyrs put together, the penances of all the monks, all the tears shed by them since the beginning of the world and all their deeds until the end of time.[7]

The Mass: The Life of Each Christian

Because the Mass is the same sacrifice as Calvary, sacramentally renewed, with all its strength and sanctifying power, the Church considers it the center of its life and the life of each of the faithful.

> The Eucharistic sacrifice is the 'source and summit of all Christian life'. It is a single sacrifice that embraces everything. It is the greatest treasure of the Church. It is her life.[8]

The Mass is also the center of the life and mission of each priest, who finds in it the direction and goal of his ministry.

> The holy Mass brings us face to face with one of the central mysteries of our faith, because it is the gift of the Blessed Trinity to the Church. It is because of this that we can consider the Mass the center and the source of a Christian's spiritual life.

> It is the aim of all the sacraments. The life of grace, into which we are brought by Baptism, and which is increased and strengthened by Confirmation, grows to its fullness in the Mass.[9]

---

7. St. John M. Vianney, Sermon on the holy Mass.
8. St. John Paul II, Prayer on Holy Thursday, 1982.
9. St. Josemaría Escrivá, *Christ Is Passing By* (=CPB) 87, Princeton, N.J.: Scepter Publishers, 1974.

The more perfect form of participation in the Mass whereby the faithful, after the priest's Communion, receive the Lord's body from the same sacrifice is warmly recommended to those who are duly prepared and in the state of grace.[10]

Since the sacrifice of the Mass is the same as the sacrifice of Calvary, their purpose is the same:

- To adore the Blessed Trinity. The sacrifice of the Cross was first of all a sacrifice of adoration and praise of God. Although the Mass is sometimes offered "in honor and in memory of the saints, the Church teaches us that the Mass is not offered to the saints but to God alone who has given them their crown."[11]

- To give thanks for the many benefits we receive from God, including those of which we are not aware. The second aim of the Mass is thanksgiving. Only Christ our Lord can offer God a worthy hymn of thanksgiving. He did so at the Last Supper when he gave thanks and when, hanging on the Cross, he continued to give thanks; our Lord continues to thank God the Father for us in the holy sacrifice of the Mass.

- To ask pardon for our sins and for the many times we have not loved God as we should. This desire for expiation and atonement should lead us to make a good confession. The same Christ who died on the Cross for our sins is present and offered in the Mass "so that sins may be forgiven."

- To ask for the spiritual and material things we need. The fourth purpose of the Mass is petition. Jesus Christ on the cross died "offering prayers and supplications and was heard because of his reverent obedience" and now in Heaven "lives always to make intercession for us."[12] These graces benefit those present at Holy Mass and the persons for whom it is offered.

---

10. Vatican Council II, *Sacrosanctum Concilium* 55.

11. Council of Trent, Session 22, chapter 3.

12. Hebrews 5: 7; 7: 25.

The Mass: External Participation

We should participate in the Mass externally, taking care of some details.

- Attend the Mass with a spirit of prayer, praying as the Church teaches us to pray, avoiding distractions. Be one with the words, actions, and gestures of the celebrant, who acts in the Person of Christ. Give up personal preferences; accept the option that the celebrant, considering the circumstances of the people in each community, has chosen from among the legitimate possibilities that the liturgy offers to us.

- Listen, respond, acclaim, sing, or keep opportune silence, in order to facilitate union with God and to deepen your reflection on the word of God.

- Stand, sit, and kneel—and be serene—even if you see someone who does not do so.

- Be punctual. This is a considerate detail for Christ our Lord, himself, and for others who are attending Mass. Arrive before the priest goes to the altar. Leave only after the priest has left.

- Use your missal, or the missalette available in the church. By following the prayers of the priest, you can avoid distractions. The more complete missals for the faithful have the prayers of the Mass distributed in three main sections: Fixed Prayers of the Order of Mass, Proper Prayers, and Readings. The missalettes for the use of the faithful usually contain some of the variable prayers for each day's Mass and most of the fixed parts of the Order of Mass arranged in their usual sequence.

- Dress properly as for an important meeting and not, for instance, as if you were going to participate in a sport. Dress ought to convey the respect, solemnity and joy of the Mass.[13]

---

13. Cf. *Catechism of the Catholic Church* (=CCC) 1387, Librería Editrice Vaticana, 1994.

The Mass: Communion and Thanksgiving

Having the right intention in receiving Communion means having these good purposes: to please God, to achieve greater union with him through charity, and to apply this divine remedy to one's moral weaknesses. The Sacrament should not be received out of routine, vainglory, or human respect. We are bound, under serious obligation, to receive Holy Communion at least once a year—ordinarily during Easter time—and when we are in danger of death.

Holy Communion may be received a second time on a given day, when and if one attends Holy Mass, or when one in danger of death receives the Blessed Sacrament as Viaticum.

- Complete the Mass with an intense thanksgiving. Devote a few minutes to private prayer. In this way, your Mass will have direct influence on your work, your family life, your dealings with others, and the manner in which you will spend the rest of your day. In short, the Mass should not be an isolated event of the day; rather, it should be the inspiration and the dynamo for all your actions.

- Turn the whole day into a continuous preparation for the holy sacrifice of the Mass—working and praying—and, at the same time, into a neverending act of thanksgiving. For a Christian, all honest activities can be turned into prayer.

- Imitate the piety of the Blessed Virgin Mary and ask it of her. While our Lord offered and immolated his flesh, Mary offered and immolated her spirit. Participate in each Mass as if it were your last.

GUIDELINES FOR RECEIVING COMMUNION

For Catholics: As Catholics, we fully participate in the celebration of the Eucharist when we receive Holy Communion. We are encouraged to receive Communion devoutly and frequently. In order to be properly disposed to receive Communion, participants should not be conscious of grave sin and normally should have fasted for one hour. A person who is conscious of grave sin is not to receive the Body and Blood of the Lord without prior sacramental confession except for a grave reason where there is no opportunity for confession. In this case, the person is to be mindful of the obligation to make an act of perfect contrition, including the intention of confessing as soon as possible (canon 916). A frequent reception of the Sacrament of Penance is encouraged for all.

For Other Christians: We welcome our fellow Christians to this celebration of the Eucharist as our brothers and sisters. We pray that our common baptism and the action of the Holy Spirit in this Eucharist will draw us closer to one another and begin to dispel the sad divisions which separate us. We pray that these will lessen and finally disappear, in keeping with Christ's prayer for us "that they may all be one" (Jn 17:21).

Because Catholics believe that the celebration of the Eucharist is a sign of the reality of the oneness of faith, life, and worship, members of those churches with whom we are not yet fully united are ordinarily not admitted to Holy Communion. Eucharistic sharing in exceptional circumstances by other Christians requires permission according to the directives of the diocesan bishop and the provisions of canon law (canon 844 § 4). Members of the Orthodox Churches, the Assyrian Church of the East, and the Polish National Catholic Church are urged to respect the discipline of their own Churches. According to Roman Catholic discipline, the Code of Canon Law does not object to the reception of communion by Christians of these Churches (canon 844 § 3).

For those not receiving Holy Communion: All who are not receiving Holy Communion are encouraged to express in their hearts a prayerful desire for unity with the Lord Jesus and with one another.

For non-Christians: We also welcome to this celebration those who do not share our faith in Jesus Christ. While we cannot admit them to Holy Communion, we ask them to offer their prayers for the peace and the unity of the human family.

PRAYERS AFTER MASS

PRAYER OF ST. THOMAS AQUINAS

Lord, holy Father, almighty and ever-living God, I thank you. For though I am a sinner and your unprofitable servant, you have fed me with the precious Body and Blood of your Son, our Lord Jesus Christ. You did this not because I deserved it, but because you are kind and merciful.

I pray that this holy Communion may not add to my guilt and punishment, but may lead me to forgiveness and salvation. May it be for me the armor of faith and the shield of good will. May it purify me from evil ways and put an end to my base passions. May it bring me charity and patience, humility and obedience, and may it strengthen my power to do every kind of good. May it be a strong defense against the deceit of all my enemies, visible and invisible. May it calm perfectly all my evil impulses, bodily and spiritual. May it unite me more closely to you, the one true God; may it bring me full possession of the goal I am longing for.

And I pray that you will lead me, a sinner, to the magnificent banquet where you, with your Son and the Holy Spirit, are for all your saints the true light, total fulfillment, everlasting joy, gladness without end, exquisite delight, and most perfect happiness. Grant this through Christ our Lord. Amen.

SELF-DEDICATION TO JESUS CHRIST

Lord, take all my freedom. Accept my memory, my understanding, and my will. You have given me all that I have or hold dear. I return it to you, that it may be governed by your will. Give me only your grace and the gift of loving you, and I will be rich enough; I will ask for nothing more. Amen.

PRAYER OF ST. BONAVENTURE

Most sweet Lord Jesus, pierce my inmost heart with the most dear and most bracing wound of your love. Pierce it with true, serene, apostolic, and most holy charity, that my soul may ever yearn and melt with love for you and the desire to possess you. May my soul be drawn toward you and overwhelmed with the hope of entering your courts. May it long to be dissolved and to be with you.

Grant that my soul may hunger for you, the Bread of angels and the food of holy souls, our supersubstantial Bread, having in itself every sweetness and good taste, having the delightfulness of all that charms my heart. May my heart always long for you, and find its nourishment in you, on whom the angels long to gaze, and may my inmost heart be filled with the sweetness of your savor. May my heart thirst for you, the fountain of life and of wisdom and of knowledge and of eternal life, the torrent of pleasure, and the richness of the house of God.

May my heart always draw near to you, seek you, catch sight of you, be drawn to you, and arrive at your presence. May my heart think of you, speak of you, and do all that it does for the glory of your name, with humility and care and affection and delight, with eagerness and with deep feeling, and with perseverance to the end. Thus may you alone always be my hope, all my confidence, my joy, my rest and my tranquility, my peace, all that charms me; my fragrance, my sweetness, my food, my nourishment, my refuge, my help, my wisdom, my portion, my possession, my treasure. In you may my mind and my heart be fixed and secure and rooted for ever without any change. Amen.

PRAYER TO OUR REDEEMER (ANIMA CHRISTI)

Soul of Christ, sanctify me.

Body of Christ, save me.

Blood of Christ, inebriate me.

Water from the side of Christ, wash me.

Passion of Christ, strengthen me.

O good Jesus, hear me.

Within your wounds, hide me.

Apart from you let me never be.

From the enemy, defend me.

In the hour of my death, call me.

And close to you bid me, that with your saints
I may always be praising you eternally. Amen.

PRAYER TO JESUS CHRIST CRUCIFIED

Look down upon me, O good
and sweetest Jesus, while before
your face I humbly kneel. Most
fervently I pray and beg you
to fix deep within my heart
lively sentiments of faith, hope,
and charity, true sorrow for
my sins, and a firm purpose of
amendment. With deep affection
and sorrow I contemplate your
five wounds. I have before my
eyes, O good Jesus, what David
the prophet spoke of you, as
though you were saying it
yourself: "They have pierced
my hands and my feet, they
have numbered all my bones"
(Ps 22 [21]:17).

THE UNIVERSAL PRAYER

Attributed to Pope Clement XI (1721-1724)

Lord, I believe in you; grant me a stronger faith. I trust in you; give me a more confident hope. I love you; may I love you more ardently. I am sorry for my sins; may I have a deeper sorrow.

I worship you as my first beginning; I long for you
as my last end. I praise you
as my constant helper and
invoke you as my gracious protector.

Guide me by your wisdom, correct me with your justice, comfort me with your kindness, protect me with your power.

I offer you, Lord, my thoughts, that they may rise to you; my words, that they may speak of you; my actions, that they may follow your will; my sufferings, that they may be borne for you.

I will whatever you will: I will all because you will it; I will all things to be as you wish them; I will them as long as you will them.

Lord, enlighten my understanding, inflame my will, purify my heart, and sanctify my soul.

Help me repent of my past sins and put to flight future temptations. Make me conquer my evil inclinations and cultivate the virtues I should have.

Grant that I may love you, O good God, and despise myself. May I have zeal for my neighbor and contempt for the world.

May I strive to obey my superiors and to assist those dependent on me; make me solicitous of my friends, and happy to spare my enemies.

Help me to master pleasure-seeking by austerity, greed by generosity, anger by gentleness, and apathy by fervor.

Make me prudent in my plans, courageous in times of danger, patient in adversity, and humble in prosperity.

Keep me, Lord, attentive at prayer, temperate in food and drink, diligent in my work, and firm in my good intentions.

Let my inner life be innocent and my outer behavior modest. Let my speech be blameless and my life well-ordered.

May I take care to master my natural impulses; let me cherish growth in grace. May I keep your laws, and come at last to win salvation.

Teach me to realize how slight are earthly things and how great is that which is divine, how swiftly things of time pass, and how enduring are eternal realities.

Help me prepare for death and have a right fear of judgment; may I escape Hell and obtain Paradise.

Grant this through Christ our Lord. Amen.

PRAYER TO THE BLESSED VIRGIN MARY

Mary, most holy virgin and mother, look down upon me! I have now received your most dear Son. You conceived him in your immaculate womb; you gave birth to him, and nursed him, and enfolded him with most loving embraces. Humbly and with love I now present to you anew this Son of yours. His very appearance brought you joy and filled you with all delight. I offer him to you, that you may hold him again in your arms and love him with all your heart. I do this as an act of worship of the most holy Trinity, and I offer him for your honor and glory, that through him my needs and those of the whole world may be fulfilled. I ask you, most dear Mother, to obtain for me forgiveness of all my sins, the grace of serving Jesus most faithfully from now on, and the gift of final perseverance, so that with you I may praise him forever. Amen.

PRAYER TO ST. MICHAEL THE ARCHANGEL

Saint Michael the Archangel, defend us in battle; be our defense against the wickedness and snares of the devil. May God rebuke him, we humbly pray. And do you, O prince of the heavenly host, by the power of God thrust into hell Satan and all the evil spirits who prowl about the world for the ruin of souls. Amen.

PRAYER TO ST. JOSEPH

Saint Joseph, father and guardian of virgins, to whose faithful
keeping Christ Jesus, innocence itself, and Mary, the Virgin of
virgins, were entrusted, I pray and beseech you by that twofold
and most precious charge, by Jesus and Mary, to save me from all
uncleanness, to keep my mind untainted, my heart pure, and my
body chaste, and to help me always to serve Jesus and Mary in
perfect chastity. Amen.

CANTICLE OF THE THREE CHILDREN

Dan 3: 57-88 and 56

Ant. Let us sing the hymn of the three children, * which these holy
ones sang of old in the fiery furnace, giving praise to the Lord.
(Easter Time Alleluia.)

1. Bless the Lord, all you works of the Lord;
   praise and exalt him above all for ever.

2. Heavens, bless the Lord;
   angels of the Lord, bless the Lord.

3. All you waters that are above the heavens,
              bless the Lord,
   let all the powers bless the Lord.

4. Sun and moon, bless the Lord;
   stars of heaven, bless the Lord.

5. Every shower and dew, bless the Lord;
   all you winds, bless the Lord.

6. Fire and heat, bless the Lord;
   cold and heat, bless the Lord.

7. Dews and hoarfrosts, bless the Lord;
   frost and cold, bless the Lord.

8. Ice and snow, bless the Lord;
   nights and days, bless the Lord.

9. Light and darkness, bless the Lord;
   lightning and clouds, bless the Lord.

10. Let the earth bless the Lord;
    let it praise and exalt him above all for ever.

11. Mountains and hills, bless the Lord;
    everything growing from the earth, bless the Lord.

12. Seas and rivers, bless the Lord;
    fountains, bless the Lord.

13. Whales and all that move in the waters, bless the Lord;
    all you fowls of the air, bless the Lord.

14. All you beasts and cattle, bless the Lord;
    sons of men, bless the Lord.

15. Israel, bless the Lord;
    praise and exalt him above all for ever.

16. Priests of the Lord, bless the Lord;
    servants of the Lord, bless the Lord.

17. Spirits and souls of the just, bless the Lord;
    holy men of humble heart, bless the Lord.

18. Ananias, Azarias and Misael, bless the Lord;
    praise and exalt him above all for ever.

19. Let us bless the Father and the Son, with the Holy Spirit;
    let us praise and exalt him above all for ever.

20. Blessed are you, Lord, in the firmament of heaven;
    and worthy of praise, and glorious above all for ever.

    Neither the **Glory be** nor **Amen** is said.

Psalm 150

1. Praise the Lord in his holy place,
   praise him in his mighty heavens.

2. Praise him for his powerful deeds,
   praise his surpassing greatness.

3. O praise him with sound of trumpet,
   praise him with lute and harp.

4. Praise him with timbrel and dance,
   praise him with strings and pipes.

5. O praise him with resounding cymbals,
   praise him with clashing of cymbals.
   Let everything that lives and breathes
          give praise to the Lord.

Glory be . . .

Ant. Let us sing the hymn of the three children, * which these holy ones sang of old in the fiery furnace, giving praise to the Lord. (Easter Time Alleluia.)

Lord, have mercy. Christ, have mercy. Lord, have mercy.
Our Father . . .

℣. And lead us not into temptation,

℟. **But deliver us from evil.**

℣. Let all your works praise you, Lord.

℟. **And let your saints bless you.**

℣. Your saints shall rejoice in glory.

℟. **They shall rejoice in their resting place.**

℣. Not unto us, Lord, not unto us,

℟. **But unto your name give glory.**

℣. O Lord, hear my prayer.

℟. **And let my cry come unto you.**

   Priests add:

℣. The Lord be with you.

℟. **And with your spirit.**

Let us pray.

God, who allayed the flames of fire for three children, grant in your mercy that the flame of vice may not consume us your servants.

Direct, we beseech you, Lord, our actions by your inspirations and further them by your assistance, so that every word and work of ours may begin always from you and by you be likewise ended.

Quench in us, we beseech you, Lord, the flame of vice, even as you enabled blessed Lawrence to overcome his fire of sufferings. Through Christ our Lord.

℟. **Amen.**

PSALM 2

This messianic psalm should inspire us with courage to persevere in spite of the attacks of the devil against the kingdom of God on earth. It also reminds us that our hope comes from our being children of God.

Ant. His kingdom is a kingdom of all ages, and all kings shall serve and obey him. (Easter Time Alleluia.)

1. Why this tumult among nations,
   among peoples this useless murmuring?

2. They arise, the kings of the earth;
   princes plot against the Lord
       and his anointed.

3. "Come, let us break their fetters;
   come, let us cast off their yoke."

4. He who sits in the heavens laughs;
   the Lord is laughing them to scorn.

5. Then he will speak in his anger,
   his rage will strike them with terror.

6. "It is I who have set up my king on Zion,
   my holy mountain."

7. I will announce the decree of the Lord:
   The Lord said to me: "You are my Son.
   It is I who have begotten you this day.

8. "Ask and I shall bequeath to you
               the nations,
   put the ends of the earth in your possession.

9. "With a rod of iron you will break them,
   shatter them like a potter's jar."

10. Now, O kings, understand;
    take warning, rulers of the earth.

11. Serve the Lord
    with awe and trembling.

12. Pay him your homage, lest he be angry and you perish, for suddenly
    his anger will blaze.
    Blessed are they
    who put their trust in God.

13. Glory be . . .

Ant. His kingdom is a kingdom of all ages, and all kings shall serve
and obey him. (Easter Time Alleluia.)

℣. O Lord, hear my prayer.

℟. **And let my cry come unto you.**

Priests add:

℣. The Lord be with you.

℟. **And with your spirit.**

Let us pray.

Almighty and eternal God, you have renewed all creation in your
beloved Son, the king of the whole universe. May all the people of
the earth, now torn apart by the wound of sin, become subject to
the gentle rule of your only-begotten Son, Who lives and reigns
with you and the Holy Spirit, one God, for ever and ever.

℟. **Amen.**

LITANY OF HUMILITY

Cardinal Merry del Val, who composed this litany, often recited it
after the celebration of the holy Mass.

O Jesus! meek and humble of heart, **Hear me.**
From the desire of being esteemed, **Deliver me, Jesus.**
From the desire of being loved…
From the desire of being extolled…
From the desire of being honored…
From the desire of being praised…
From the desire of being preferred to others…
From the desire of being consulted…
From the desire of being approved…
From the fear of being humiliated…
From the fear of being despised…
From the fear of suffering rebukes…
From the fear of being calumniated…
From the fear of being forgotten…
From the fear of being ridiculed…
From the fear of being wronged…
From the fear of being suspected…
That others may be loved more than I,

Jesus, grant me the grace to desire it.

That others may be esteemed more than I…
That in the opinion of the world
    others may increase and I may decrease…
That others may be chosen and I set aside…
That others may be praised and I unnoticed…
That others may be preferred to me in everything…
That others become holier than I, provided that
    I may become as holy as I should…

EUCHARISTIC ADORATION

The Catholic Church has always displayed and still displays this latria that ought to be paid to the Sacrament of the Eucharist, both during Mass and outside of it by taking the greatest possible care of the consecrated Hosts by exposing them to the solemn veneration of the faithful, and carrying them about in procession.

The tabernacle was first intended for the reservation of the Eucharist in a worthy place so that it could be brought to the sick and those absent, outside of Mass. As faith in the Real Presence of Christ in his Eucharist deepened, the Church became conscious of the meaning of silent adoration of the Lord present under the Eucharistic species. It is for this reason that the tabernacle should be located in an especially worthy place in the church and should be constructed in such a way that it emphasizes and manifests the truth of the Real Presence of Christ in the Blessed Sacrament.

It is highly fitting that Christ should have wanted to remain present to his Church in this unique way. Since Christ was about to take his departure from his own visible form, he wanted to give us his sacramental presence; since he was about to offer himself on the Cross to save us, he wanted us to have the memorial of the love with which he loved us 'to the end' (Jn 13:1), even to the giving of his life. In his Eucharistic presence... he remains under signs that express and communicate this love:

"The Church and the world have a great need for Eucharistic worship. Jesus awaits us in this sacrament of love. Let us be generous with our time in going to meet Him in adoration and in contemplation that is full of faith, and ready to make reparation for the serious offenses and crimes of the world. Let our adoration never cease."[1]

EXPOSITION AND BENEDICTION OF THE BLESSED SACRAMENT

"Toward the beginning of the thirteenth century, great emphasis was being placed on the truth of the Real Presence of Christ in the Blessed Sacrament. Although Catholics had always believed that

---

1. CCC 1379-1380.

Jesus is actually present in the Eucharist, the fact was now being stressed to counteract some false ideas that were prevalent at the time. To correct mistaken notions and even superstition in regard to the doctrine, the Church fostered a renewal of faith in and devotion toward the Real Presence. In 1264, the feast of Corpus Christi, honoring the Body of our Lord, was established. Also in this period, St.Thomas Aquinas, the Angelic Doctor, composed his beautiful hymns praising the Holy Eucharist.[2]

O Salutaris Hostia / O Saving Victim

O salutáris Hóstia,
Quæ cæli pandis óstium:
Bella premunt hostília,
Da robur, fer auxílium.

O Saving Victim opening wide
The gates of heav'n to man below!
Our foes press on from every side;
Thine aid supply, Thy strength bestow.

Uni trinóque Dómino
Sit sempitérna glória,
Qui vitam sine término,
Nobis donet in pátria.
Amen.

To Thy great name be endless praise,
Immortal Godhead, One in Three;
O, grant us endless length of days,
In our true native land with Thee.
Amen.

Or: I Devoutly Adore You (p. 75)

Pange, Lingua / Sing, My Tongue

Pange, lingua, gloriósi
Córporis mystérium,
Sanguinísque pretiósi,
Quem in mundi prétium,
Fructus ventris generósi
Rex effúdit géntium.

Sing, my tongue, the Savior's glory,
Of his flesh the mystery sing,
Of the blood, all price exceeding,
Shed by our immortal King,
Destined, for the world's redemption,
From a noble womb to spring.

Nobis datus, nobis natus
Ex intácta Vírgine,
Et in mundo conversátus,
Sparso verbi sémine,
Sui moras incolátus
Miro clausit órdine.

Of a pure and spotless Virgin
Born for us on earth below,
He, as man with man conversing,
Stayed, the seeds of truth to sow;
Then he closed in solemn order
Wondrously his life of woe.

---

2. Anthony Teolis, "Mary at Benediction," *Homiletic and Pastoral Review*, vol. XCVII, no. 2, p. 54.

In suprémæ nocte cœnæ
Recúmbens cum frátribus,
Observáta lege plene
Cibis in legálibus,
Cibum turbæ duodénæ
Se dat suis mánibus.

On the night of that last supper,
Seated with his chosen band,
He the paschal victim eating,
First fulfills the law's command;
Then as food to all his brethren,
Gives himself with his own hand.

Verbum caro, panem verum
Verbo carnem éfficit:
Fitque sanguis
    Christi merum,
Et, si sensus déficit,
Ad firmándum cor sincérum
Sola fides súfficit.

Word made flesh, the bread of nature
By his word to flesh he turns;
Wine into his blood he changes:
What though sense
    no change discerns?
Only be the heart in earnest,
Faith her lesson quickly learns.

Tantum ergo sacraméntum
Venerémur cérnui,
Et antíquum documéntum
Novo cedat rítui:
Præstet fides suppleméntum
Sensuum deféctui.

Down in adoration falling,
Lo, the sacred Host we hail;
Lo, o'er ancient forms departing
Newer rites of grace prevail;
Faith for all defects supplying
Where the feeble senses fail.

Genitóri, Genitóque
Laus et iubilátio,
Salus, honor, virtus quoque
Sit et benedíctio:
Procedénti ab utróque
Compar sit laudátio.
Amen.

To the everlasting Father,
And the Son who reigns on high,
With the Holy Spirit proceeding
Forth from each eternally,
Be salvation, honor, blessing,
Might, and endless majesty.
Amen.

℣. You have given them bread from heaven. (Easter Time Alleluia.)

℟. Having all sweetness within it (Easter Time Alleluia.)

Let us pray.

Lord Jesus Christ, you gave us the eucharist as the memorial of your
suffering and death. May our worship of this sacrament of your
body and blood help us to experience the salvation you won for us
and the peace of the kingdom where you live with the Father and
the Holy Spirit, one God, for ever and ever.

℟. Amen.

Then the priest or deacon makes the Sign of the Cross over the people with the monstrance or ciborium, in silence. The Divine Praises may be said:

Blessed be God.

Blessed be his holy name.

Blessed be Jesus Christ, true God and true man.

Blessed be the name of Jesus.

Blessed be his most Sacred Heart.

Blessed be his most Precious Blood.

Blessed be Jesus in the most holy Sacrament of the Altar.

Blessed be the Holy Spirit, the Paraclete.

Blessed be the great Mother of God, Mary most holy.

Blessed be her holy and Immaculate Conception.

Blessed be her glorious Assumption.

Blessed be the name of Mary, virgin and mother.

Blessed be St. Joseph, her most chaste spouse.

Blessed be God in his angels and in his saints. Amen.

At this moment, the pious custom of reciting the Prayer of Reparation to the Eucharistic Heart of Jesus may be observed.

May the Heart of Jesus in the Most Blessed Sacrament be praised, adored, and loved with grateful affection at every moment in all the tabernacles of the world, now and until the end of time. Amen.

After that, the priest or deacon who gave the blessing, or another priest or deacon, replaces the Blessed Sacrament in the tabernacle and genuflects. Meanwhile, the people may sing:

O Sacrament most holy,
O Sacrament divine,
All praise and all thanksgiving
Be every moment Thine.

or:

Holy God, we praise thy name;
Lord of all, we bow before thee!
All on earth thy scepter claim,
All in heav'n above adore thee;

Infinite thy vast domain,
Everlasting is thy reign. (Repeat these two lines)

GUIDE FOR MAKING A HOLY HOUR BEFORE THE BLESSED SACRAMENT

The devotion of making a Holy Hour—spending an hour in prayer before the Blessed Sacrament—is becoming more and more widespread among Catholics. The goal of this devotion is to adore Jesus Christ truly present in the Sacred Host and at the same time to contemplate his unconditional love so magnificently manifested in this Bread of Life. Before making a Holy Hour, it is good to have a plan to use this time fruitfully. Time spent before the Lord could include expressing your inner sentiments and struggles, meditating on a passage from Scripture perhaps with the aid of a spiritual book, and bringing petitions and requests to the Lord. The Holy Hour could include prayers of adoration, thanksgiving, petition, and contrition.

Preparation

Before beginning a Holy Hour, prepare yourself by acknowledging the presence of Christ in the Blessed Sacrament, and ask him to make your time of prayer fruitful. It is also good to ask for the intercession of Our Lady, who can bring you into a closer relationship with her Son.

Prayer Before Making a Holy Hour

"My Lord and my God, I firmly believe that you are here, that you see me, that you hear me. I adore you with profound reverence; I ask your pardon for my sins and the grace to make this time of prayer fruitful. My immaculate Mother, Saint Joseph my father and lord, my guardian angel, intercede for me."

Some other useful prayers are:

- Spiritual Communion (p. 76)
- Morning Offering (p. 35)
- Consecration to the Blessed Virgin Mary (p. 35)

Adoration

Adoration is worship and veneration given to God because of his eternal and infinite goodness. It recognizes God as the source of all goodness, who enjoys infinite transcendence above every creature. An excellent prayer and a well known litany of adoration are:

- I Devoutly Adore You (*Adoro Te Devote*) (p. 75)
- Litany of the Sacred Heart of Jesus (p. 105)

Thanksgiving

Prayers of thanksgiving show gratitude to God for his infinite love and for filling every person's life with every good thing, both material and spiritual. Some excellent prayers of thanksgiving are:

- The Te Deum (p. 89)
- The Magnificat (p. 173)

Petition

Prayers of petition request favor and blessings from God for oneself and for others. It is assured God will honor every request by either granting what is asked for or giving something even more beneficial for the soul. Some prayers of petition could include:

- The Universal Prayer (p. 60)
- Prayer for the Pope (p. 35)

Atonement

In prayers of atonement, the petitioner asks God to grant his mercy and forgiveness. Some examples of prayers of atonement include:

- Prayer to Jesus Christ Crucified (p. 59)
- The Confiteor (p. 41)
- The Act of Contrition (p. 41)
- Acceptance of Death (p. 122)

A Holy Hour is also an excellent opportunity to pray the Holy Rosary (p. 149), which is a meditation on the mysteries of the life of Christ, and the Stations of the Cross (p. 107), which is a meditation on the Passion and Death of Our Lord.

Finally, it is fitting to finish the Holy Hour with a prayer thanking God for all the blessing he has bestowed in this time of prayer. A good way to conclude is the short prayer "Jesus, Mary, and Joseph" (p. 42).

Prayer After Making a Holy Hour

"I thank you, my God, for the good resolutions, affections, and inspirations that you have communicated to me in this meditation. I ask your help to put them into effect. My immaculate Mother, Saint Joseph my father and lord, my guardian angel, intercede for me."

I DEVOUTLY ADORE YOU (ADORO TE DEVOTE)

I devoutly adore you, O hidden God,
truly hidden beneath these appearances.
My whole heart submits to you
and in contemplating you it surrenders itself completely.

Sight, touch, taste are all deceived in their judgment of you,
but hearing suffices firmly to believe.
I believe all that the Son of God has spoken:
there is nothing truer than this word of Truth.

On the cross only the Divinity was hidden,
but here the humanity is also hidden.
I believe and confess both,
and I ask for what the repentant thief asked.

I do not see the wounds as Thomas did,
but I confess that you are my God.
Make me believe in you more and more,
hope in you, and love you.

O Memorial of our Lord's Death!
Living bread that gives life to man,
grant my soul to live on you
and always to savor your sweetness.

Lord Jesus, good Pelican,
wash me clean with your Blood,
one drop of which can free
the entire world of all its sins.

Jesus, whom now I see hidden,
I ask you to fulfill what I so desire:
that on seeing you face to face,
I may be happy in seeing your glory. Amen.

VISIT TO THE BLESSED SACRAMENT

"When the faithful adore Christ present in the sacrament, they should remember that his presence derives from the sacrifice and is directed towards both sacramental and spiritual communion." I therefore encourage Christians regularly to visit Christ present in the Blessed Sacrament of the altar, for we are all called to abide in the presence of God, thanks to him who is with us until the end of time. In contemplation, Christians will perceive ever more profoundly that the paschal mystery is at the heart of all Christian life. This practice leads them to join more intensely in the paschal mystery and to make the Eucharistic sacrifice, the perfect gift, the center of their life in accordance with their specific vocation, for it "confers an incomparable dignity upon the Christian people."[3]

Jesus has remained in the Sacred Host for us so as to stay by our side, to sustain us, to guide us. And love can only be repaid with love.

How could we not turn to the Blessed Sacrament each day, even if it is only for a few minutes, to bring him our greetings and our love as children and as brothers?[4]

Recite three times:

℣. Adorémus in ætérnum Sanctíssimum Sacraméntum.

℟. **Adorémus in ætérnum Sanctíssimum Sacraméntum.**

Pater Noster… Ave María… Gloria Patri…

℣. Let us for ever adore the most holy Sacrament.

℟. **Let us for ever adore the most holy Sacrament.**

Our Father… Hail Mary… Glory be…

Spiritual Communion

I wish, my Lord, to receive you with the purity, humility, and devotion with which your most holy Mother received you, with the spirit and fervor of the saints.

---

3. St. John Paul II, Letter to Bishop Albert Houssiau of Liege on 28 May 1996, IWEM 50; MF 67.
4. FW 686.

GUIDE FOR A GOOD CONFESSION

"To those who have been far away from the Sacrament of Reconciliation and forgiving love, I make this appeal: *Come back to this source of grace; do not be afraid!* Christ himself is waiting for you. He will heal you, and you will be at peace with God!"[1]

The basic requirement for a good confession is to have the intention of returning to God like the *Prodigal Son* and of acknowledging our sins with true sorrow before his representative, the priest.

Examination of Conscience

Examine your conscience. Recall your sins. Calmly ask yourself what you have done with full knowledge and full consent against God's Commandments.

THE FIRST COMMANDMENT

* Did I perform my duties toward God reluctantly or grudgingly?

* Did I neglect my prayer life? Did I recite my usual prayers?

* Did I receive Holy Communion in the state of mortal sin or without the necessary preparation?

* Did I violate the one-hour Eucharistic fast?

* Did I fail to mention some grave sin in my previous confessions?

* Did I seriously believe in something superstitious or engage in a superstitious practice (e.g., crystals, palm-reading, fortune telling, or Ouija boards)?

* Did I seriously doubt a matter of faith?

* Did I show my Catholic identity when dealing with others?

* Did I put my faith in danger—without a good reason—by accessing the Internet; reading a book, pamphlet, or magazine;

---

1. Homily of Pope St. John Paul II on September 13, 1987, at Westover Hills, San Antonio, Texas.

or viewing movies and television programs that contain material contrary to Catholic faith or morals?

- Did I endanger my faith by joining, or attending meetings of, organizations opposed to the Catholic faith (non-catholic denominations, the Communist Party, Freemasonry, "new age" cults, or other religions)? Did I without a legitimate reason take part in one of its activities?

- Have I committed the sin of sacrilege (profanation of a sacred person, place, or thing)?

THE SECOND COMMANDMENT

- Did I fail to try my best to fulfill the promises and resolutions that I made to God?

- Did I take the name of God in vain? Did I make use of God's name mockingly, jokingly, angrily, or in any other irreverent manner?

- Did I make use of the Blessed Virgin Mary's name or another saint's name mockingly, jokingly, angrily, or in any other irreverent manner?

- Have I been a sponsor in Baptism or participated actively in other religious ceremonies outside the Catholic Church?

- Did I tell a lie under oath?

THE THIRD COMMANDMENT

- Did I miss Mass on a Sunday or a Holy Day of Obligation without a legitimate reason?

- Did I fail to dress appropriately for Mass?

- Have I, without sufficient reason, arrived at Mass so late that I failed to fulfill the Sunday or Holy Day of Obligation?

- Did I allow myself to be distracted during Mass, by not paying attention, by looking around out of curiosity, etc.?

- Did I cause another to be distracted?

- Have I without a sufficiently good reason performed any work or business activity that would inhibit the worship due to God, the joy proper to the Lord's Day, or the appropriate relaxation of mind and body, on a Sunday or a Holy Day of Obligation?

- Did I fail to generously help the Church in her necessities in accord with my ability?

- Did I fail to fast or abstain on a day for which this is prescribed by the Church?

THE FOURTH COMMANDMENT

- Was I disobedient toward my parents or others in authority?

- Did I neglect to help my parents when my help was needed?

- Did I treat my parents and teachers with affection and respect?

- Did I react proudly when I was corrected?

- Did I help out at home?

THE FIFTH COMMANDMENT

- Did I easily get angry or lose my temper?

- Was I envious or jealous of others?

- Did I injure, or take the life of, anyone? Was I ever reckless or under the influence of alcohol or drugs when driving?

- Was I an occasion of sin for others by way of conversation, the telling of jokes religiously, racially, or sexually offensive, my way of dressing, inviting somebody to attend certain shows, recommending inappropriate or immoral Web sites on the Internet, lending harmful books or magazines, helping someone to steal, etc.? Did I give scandal to others? Did I try to repair the damage done by the scandal I gave?

- Did I lead others to sin? What sin or sins were involved?

- Did I neglect my health by failing to maintain a healthy lifestyle to the detriment or the neglect of my physical health? Did I attempt to take my life?

- Did I harm myself or another?

- Did I get drunk or use prohibited drugs?

- Did I eat or drink more than a sufficient amount, allowing myself to get carried away by gluttony? Did I crave a certain food or drink to excess?

- Did I participate in any form of physical violence?

- Did I consent to, advise, or actively take part in an abortion? Was I aware that the Church punishes with automatic excommunication (*latæ sententiæ*) those who *procure and achieve* abortion? Do I realize that this is a very grave sin?

- Did I consent to, advise, or actively take part in euthanasia? Do I realize that "an act or omission which, of itself or by intention, causes death in order to eliminate suffering constitutes a murder gravely contrary to the dignity of the human person and to the respect due to the living God, his creator"?[2]

- Did I support a public official who openly supports abortion?

- Did I cause harm to anyone with my words, communications, or actions?

- Did I desire revenge or harbor enmity, hatred, or ill feelings when someone offended me?

- Did I ask pardon whenever I offended anyone?

- Did I insult or offensively tease others?

- Did I quarrel needlessly with others?

- Have I used my mobile phone excessively? Has it been an occasion of sin for myself or for others?

- Have I spent too much time on the Internet? Has it caused me to neglect my duties, or has it been an occasion of sin for myself or for others?

THE SIXTH AND NINTH COMMANDMENTS

- Did I willfully entertain impure thoughts?

- Did I consent to desires against the virtue of purity, even though I may not have carried them out? Were there any circumstances that aggravated the sin such as a marriage or someone's consecration to God?

- Did I engage in impure conversations? Did I start them?

- Did I look for fun in forms of entertainment that placed me in proximate occasions of sin, such as certain dances, movies, shows, books, or on the Internet with immoral content? Did I go to places where immoral conduct was taking place?

- Did I place myself in a proximate occasion of sin, such as sharing a room with a person I find sexually attractive or being alone with such a person in other circumstances that could lead to sin?

- Did I fail to take care of those details of modesty and decency that are the safeguards of purity?

- Did I fail, before watching a movie, going to a show, or reading a book, to find out its moral implications so as not to put myself in immediate danger of sin and to avoid distorting my conscience?

- Did I willfully look at pornography or other indecent pictures or cast an impure look upon myself or another? Did I willfully desire to commit such a sin?

- Did I lead others to sins of impurity or immodesty? What sins?

- Did I commit an impure act? By myself, through masturbation (which is an intrinsically and gravely disordered action)? With someone else? How many times? With someone of the same or opposite sex? Was there any circumstance of relationship (such as affinity) that could have given the sin special gravity?

- Do I have friendships that are habitual occasions of sexual sins? Am I prepared to end them?

- In courtship, is true love my fundamental reason for wanting to be with the other person? Do I constantly and cheerfully make the sacrifice of not putting the person I love in danger of sinning? Do I degrade human love by confusing it with selfishness or mere pleasure?

- Did I engage in acts such as passionate kisses, improper touches, or prolonged embraces?

- Did I look at pornography on the Internet, in magazines, or in other formats?

- Have I engaged in premarital sex?

- Did I willfully entertain impure thoughts? If any came to mind, did I fail to reject them immediately?

(FOR MARRIED PEOPLE)

- Did I, without serious reason, deprive my spouse of the marital right? Did I claim my own rights in a way which showed no concern for my spouse's state of mind or health? Did I violate conjugal fidelity in desire or in deed?

- Did I use a birth-control pill or an artificial birth control device (e.g., condom) before or after new life had already been conceived?

- Did I without grave reason, with the intention of avoiding conception, make use of marriage on only those days when offspring would not likely be engendered?

- Did I suggest to another person the use of birth-control pills or another artificial method of preventing pregnancy (e.g., a condom)?

- Did I have a hand in contributing to the *contraceptive mentality* by my advice, jokes, or attitudes?

(On abortion, contraception, sterilization, etc., cf. THE FIFTH COMMANDMENT.)

THE SEVENTH AND TENTH COMMANDMENTS

- Did I steal? What object did I steal? How much money, or how much was the object worth? Did I give it back, or at least have the intention of doing so? Did I knowingly accept stolen goods or services (cable television, Internet access) without payment?

- Have I done or caused damage to another person's property? To what extent?

- Did I harm anyone by deception or fraud?

- Did I unnecessarily spend beyond my means? Do I spend money because of vanity or caprice?

- Do I help the poor, according to my capacity?

- Was I envious of my neighbor's goods or lifestyle?

- Did I neglect to pay my debts, whether obligatory or personal?

- Did I willfully entertain a desire to steal?

- Did I give in to excessive laziness or love of comfort rather than diligently working or studying?

- Was I greedy? Do I have a materialistic view of life? Did I buy things I do not really need?

- Do I show respect for the integrity of creation? Did I show concern for the quality of life of my neighbor, including generations to come?

- Do I want to impress others with my material possessions?

THE EIGHTH COMMANDMENT

- Did I tell lies? Did I repair any damage that may have resulted from this?

- Have I unjustly or rashly accused others?

- Did I sin by detraction, that is, by telling the faults of another person without necessity?

- Did I sin by calumny, that is, by telling derogatory lies about another person?

- Did I engage in gossip, backbiting, or taletelling?

- Did I reveal a secret without due cause?

- Did I cheat on my exams, homework, or other assignments?

- Did I neglect my obligation to study? Did I neglect my responsibility to prepare myself for my future and professional life?

- Did I fail in my responsibility to show gratitude I owe to my parents and others who enable me to receive an education?

- Did I cheat on my time sheets or waste my time at work?

- Did I take company property for my own personal use?

Shorter Examination of Conscience

- When was my last good confession? Did I receive Communion or other Sacraments while in the state of mortal sin? Did I intentionally fail to confess some mortal sin in my previous confession?

- Did I willfully and seriously doubt my faith, or put myself in danger of losing it by reading literature hostile to Catholic teachings or by getting involved with non-Catholic sects? Did I engage in superstitious activities: palm reading, fortune telling?

- Did I take the name of God in vain? Did I curse or take a false oath? Did I use bad language?

- Did I miss Mass on a Sunday or a Holy Day of Obligation through my own fault, without any serious reason? Did I fast and abstain on the prescribed days?

- Did I disobey my parents or lawful superiors in important matters?

- Was I selfish in how I treated others, especially my spouse, my brothers and sisters, my other relatives, or my friends? Did I hatefully quarrel with anyone, or intentionally seek or desire revenge? Did I refuse to forgive? Did I cause physical injury or even death? Did I get drunk? Did I take illicit drugs? Did I consent to, advise, or actively take part in an abortion or in euthanasia?

- Did I willfully look at indecent pictures or watch immoral movies? Did I read immoral books or magazines? Did I engage in impure jokes or conversations? Did I willfully entertain impure thoughts or feelings? Did I commit impure acts, alone or with others? Did I take contraceptive or abortifacient pills, or use other artificial means in order to prevent conception?

- Did I steal or damage another's property? How much? Have I made reparation for the damages done? Have I been honest in my business relations?

- Did I tell lies? Did I sin by slander? By detraction—revealing unknown grave faults of others without necessity? Did I judge others rashly in serious matters? Have I tried to make restitution for any damage of reputation that I have caused?

If you remember other serious sins besides those indicated here, include them also in your confession.

Before Confession

Be truly sorry for your sins.

On the part of the penitent, the essential act of Penance is *contrition*—a clear and decisive rejection of each sin committed—together with a resolution not to commit it again, which arises from the love one has for God (this is reborn with repentance). "Understood in this way, *contrition* is, therefore, the beginning and the heart of *conversion*, of that evangelical *metanoia* which brings the person back to God like the Prodigal Son returning to his father, and which has in the sacrament of Penance its visible sign, and which perfects attrition."[3] (Attrition is imperfect contrition—the contrition born of the consideration of sin's ugliness or the fear of eternal damnation and the other penalties threatening the sinner…"[4])

The *resolution to avoid committing these sins in the future* (amendment) is the sure sign that your repentance is genuine and authentic.

This does not mean that one has to promise never to fall again into sin. A resolution to try to avoid the near occasions of sin suffices for true repentance. God's grace, in cooperation with your intention to rectify your life, will give you the strength to resist and overcome temptation in the future.

ACT OF CONTRITION

O my God,
I am heartily sorry for having offended you,
and I detest all my sins,
because I dread the loss of heaven
and the pains of hell;
but most of all because they offend you, my God, who are all
good and deserving of all my love.
I firmly resolve, with the help of your grace,
to confess my sins, to do penance,
and to amend my life. Amen.

Or:

My God,
I am sorry for my sins with all my heart.
In choosing to do wrong
and failing to do good,
I have sinned against you,
whom I should love above all things.
I firmly intend, with your help,
to do penance, to sin no more,
and to avoid whatever leads me to sin.
Our Savior Jesus Christ
suffered and died for us.
In his name, my God, have mercy.

Or:

I confess (p. 41).

You are now ready to go to confession. The rite is presented on page **88**.

During Confession

* You can begin your confession by making the Sign of the Cross and greeting the priest: **"Bless me, Father, for I have sinned."**

* The priest gives you a blessing. One response you might give is these words St. Peter said to Christ: **"Lord, you know all things; you know that I love you"** (Jn 21: 17). One then continues with the time since one's last confession: **"My last good confession was … [the approximate number of weeks, months, or years]."**

* *Say the sins that you remember.* Start with the one that is most difficult to say; after this it will be easier to mention the rest. If you received general absolution, tell this to the priest and mention the sins forgiven then.

* If you do not know how to confess, or you feel uneasy or ashamed, simply ask the priest to assist you. Be assured that he will help you to make a good confession. Simply answer his questions without hiding anything out of shame or fear. Place your trust in God: he is your merciful Father and wants to forgive you.

- If you do not remember any serious sins, be sure to confess at least some of your venial sins, adding at the end: **"I am sorry for these and all the sins of my past life, especially for…"** (mention in general any past sin for which you are particularly sorry; for example, "all my sins against charity.")

- The priest will assign you some penance and give you some advice to help you to be a better Christian.

- Listen to the words of absolution attentively. At the end answer: **"Amen."** Be willing to do the penance as soon as possible. This *penance* will diminish the temporal punishment due to sins already forgiven.

After Confession

- *Give thanks* to God for having forgiven you once again.

- Promptly and devoutly *fulfill the penance* given by the priest. Although you may receive Holy Communion even before performing your penance, it is advisable to do it as soon as possible. Penance, prayer, and other pious practices (e.g., charitable acts, monetary donations, pilgrimages) will help remit the temporal punishment due to sins already forgiven.

- If you *recall some serious sin* that you forgot to tell, rest assured that it has been forgiven with the others, but be sure to include it in your next confession.

Rite of Reconciliation

After the customary greetings, the penitent crosses himself as the priest says:

**In the name of the Father, and of the Son,
and of the Holy Spirit. Amen.**

The penitent answers:　**Amen.**

The priest may say:

May the Lord be in your heart
and help you to confess your sins with true sorrow.

Either the priest or the penitent may read or say by heart some words taken from the holy Scripture about the mercy of God and repentance, e.g.:

"Lord, you know all things; you know that I love you"
(Jn 21: 17).

The penitent accuses himself of his sins. The priest gives opportune advice, imposes the penance on him, and invites the penitent to manifest his contrition. The penitent may say:

Lord Jesus, Son of God, have mercy on me, a sinner.

The priest gives him the absolution:

God, the Father of mercies, through the death and resurrection of his Son has reconciled the world to himself and sent the Holy Spirit among us for the forgiveness of sins; through the ministry of the Church, may God give you pardon and peace, and I absolve you from your sins in the name of the Father, and of the Son, ✠ and of the Holy Spirit.

The penitent answers:　**Amen.**

The priest may dismiss the penitent with this or any other formulæ:

May the Passion of our Lord Jesus Christ, the intercession of the Blessed Virgin Mary and of all the saints, and whatever good you do and suffering you endure heal your sins, help you to grow in holiness, and reward you with eternal life.
Go in peace.

The penitent should fulfill the penance imposed.

DEVOTIONS TO
THE BLESSED TRINITY

The mystery of the Most Holy Trinity is the central mystery of Christian faith and life. It is the mystery of God in himself. It is therefore the source of all the other mysteries of faith, the light that enlightens them. It is the most fundamental and essential teaching in the "hierarchy of the truths of faith." The whole history of salvation is identical with the history of the way and the means by which the one true God, Father, Son, and Holy Spirit, reveals himself to men "and reconciles and unites with himself those who turn away from sin."[1]

Christians are baptized "in the name of the Father and of the Son and of the Holy Spirit." Before receiving the Sacrament they respond to a three-part question when asked to confess the Father, the Son, and the Spirit: "I do." "The faith of all Christians rests on the Trinity."[2]

TE DEUM

This hymn of praise can be traced back to the first centuries of Christendom. During the Middle Ages it was ascribed to Sts. Ambrose and Augustine, but it has also been attributed to Bishop Nicetas of Remesiana. Since the sixth century, it has been recited as part of the Divine Office.

1. Te Deum laudámus: *
   te Dóminum confitémur.

2. Te ætérnum Patrem, *
   omnis terra venerátur.

3. Tibi omnes ángeli, *
   tibi cæli et univérsæ
   potestátes:

1. We praise you, O God, we
   acknowledge you to be the
   Lord.

2. You, the Father everlasting, all
   the earth does worship.

3. To you all the angels,
   to you the heavens,
   and all the powers,

---

1. CCC 234; GCD 43, 47.
2. CCC 232; St. Caesarius of Arles, Sermo 9, Exp. symb.: CCL 103, 47.

4. Tibi chérubim et
   séraphim* incessábili
   voce proclámant:

4. To you the cherubim
   and seraphim cry out
   without ceasing:

5. Sanctus,* sanctus,* sanctus*
   Dóminus Deus Sábaoth.

5. Holy, holy, holy,
   Lord God of hosts.

6. Pleni sunt cæli et terra*
   maiestátis glóriæ tuæ.

6. Heaven and earth are full
   of the majesty of your glory.

7. Te gloriósus*
   apostolórum chorus,

7. You the glorious
   choir of the apostles,

8. Te prophetárum*
   laudábilis númerus,

8. You the admirable
   company of the prophets,

9. Te mártyrum candidátus*
   laudat exércitus.

9. You the white-robed army
   of martyrs do praise.

10. Te per orbem terrárum*
    sancta confitétur
    Ecclésia,

10. You the holy Church
    throughout the world
    confesses:

11. Patrem*
    imménsæ maiestátis;

11. The Father, of
    incomprehensible majesty;

12. Venerándum tuum verum*
    et únicum Fílium;

12. Your adorable, true,
    and only Son,

13. Sanctum quoque*
    Paráclitum Spíritum.

13. And the Holy Spirit,
    the Paraclete.

14. Tu rex glóriæ,*
    Christe.

14. You, O Christ,
    are the King of glory.

15. Tu Patris*
    sempitérnus es Fílius.

15. You are the everlasting
    Son of the Father.

16. Tu, ad liberándum
    susceptúrus hóminem,*
    non horruísti Vírginis úterum.

16. Having taken it upon yourself
    to free man, you did not
    disdain the Virgin's womb.

17. Tu, devícto mortis
    acúleo,* aperuísti
    credéntibus regna
    cælórum.

17. Having overcome the sting
    of death, you have opened
    to believers the Kingdom
    of Heaven.

18. Tu ad déxteram
Dei sedes * in
glória Patris.

18. You sit at the right hand
of God, in the glory of
the Father.

19. Iudex credéris *
esse ventúrus.

19. You—we do believe this—
are the Judge to come.

20. Te ergo quæsumus,
tuis fámulis súbveni, *
quos pretióso
sánguine redemísti.

20. We beseech you, therefore, to
help your servants
whom you have redeemed
with your precious Blood.

21. Ætérna fac cum
sanctis tuis * in
glória numerári.

21. Make them to be
numbered with your
saints in glory everlasting.

22. Salvum fac pópulum
tuum, Dómine, * et
bénedic hereditáti tuæ.

22. O Lord, save your
people, and bless
your inheritance.

23. Et rege eos, * et extólle
illos usque in ætérnum.

23. And govern them,
and exalt them for ever.

24. Per síngulos dies *
benedícimus te;

24. Day by day
we bless you.

25. Et laudámus nomen
tuum in sæculum, * et
in sæculum sæculi.

25. And we praise your
name for ever; yes,
for ever and ever.

26. Dignáre, Dómine, die isto *
sine peccáto nos custodíre.

26. Vouchsafe, O Lord, this day,
to keep us without sin.

27. Miserére nostri, Dómine, *
miserére nostri.

27. Have mercy on us, O Lord;
have mercy on us.

28. Fiat misericórdia tua, Dómine,
super nos, * quemádmodum
sperávimus in te.

28. Let your mercy, O Lord,
be upon us; as we have
trusted in you.

29. In te, Dómine, sperávi: *
non confúndar
in ætérnum.

29. In you, O Lord, have I
trusted: let me not be
confounded for ever.

℣. Benedíctus es, Dómine, Deus patrum nostrórum.

℟. **Et laudábilis, et gloriósus et superexaltátus in sæcula.**

℣. Benedicámus Patrem, et Fílium cum Sancto Spíritu.

℟. **Laudémus, et superexaltémus eum in sæcula.**

℣. Benedíctus es, Dómine, in firmaménto cæli.

℟. **Et laudábilis, et gloriósus, et superexaltátus in sæcula.**

℣. Bénedic, ánima mea, Dómino.

℟. **Et noli oblivísci omnes retributiónes eius.**

℣. Dómine, exáudi oratiónem meam.

℟. **Et clamor meus ad te véniat.**

Sacerdotes addunt:

℣. Dóminus vobíscum.

℟. **Et cum spíritu tuo.**

Orémus.

Deus, cuius misericórdiæ non est númerus, et bonitátis infinítus est thesáurus: piíssimæ Maiestáti tuæ pro collátis donis grátias ágimus, tuam semper cleméntiam exorántes;

℣. Blessed are you, O Lord, the God of our fathers.

℟. **And worthy to be praised, and glorified for ever.**

℣. Let us bless the Father, and the Son, with the Holy Spirit.

℟. **Let us praise and exalt him for ever.**

℣. Blessed are you, O Lord, in the firmament of heaven.

℟. **And worthy of praise, and glorious, and exalted above all for ever.**

℣. Bless the Lord, O my soul.

℟. **And forget not all his benefits.**

℣. O Lord, hear my prayer.

℟. **And let my cry come unto you.**

Priests add:

℣. The Lord be with you.

℟. **And with your spirit.**

Let us pray.

O God, of your mercies there is no number, and of your goodness the treasure is infinite; we render thanks to your most gracious majesty for the gifts you have bestowed upon us, evermore imploring your clemency that as you grant the

ut, qui peténtibus postuláta concédis, eósdem non déserens, ad præmia futúra dispónas.

Deus, qui corda fidélium Sancti Spíritus illustratióne docuísti: da nobis in eódem Spíritu recta sápere; et de eius semper consolatióne gaudére.

Deus, qui néminem in te sperántem nímium afflígi permíttis, sed pium précibus præstas audítum: pro postulatiónibus nostris, votísque suscéptis grátias ágimus, te piíssime deprecántes; ut a cunctis semper muniámur advérsis. Per Christum Dóminum nostrum.

℟. **Amen.**

petitions of them that ask you, you may never forsake them, but may prepare them for the rewards to come.

O God, who have taught the hearts of the faithful by the light of the Holy Spirit, grant us, by the same Spirit, to relish what is right, and evermore to rejoice in his consolation.

O God, who suffer none that hope in you to be afflicted beyond their strength, but listen graciously to their prayers, we render you thanks, because you have received our supplications and vows; and we most humbly beseech you that we may evermore be protected from all adversities. Through Christ our Lord.

℟. **Amen.**

ATHANASIAN CREED

Taking its name from St. Athanasius (+373), even though it is no longer attributed to him, this prayer enumerates the essential doctrines of Christianity, especially the mysteries of the Holy Trinity. St. Teresa of Avila recounts a meditation on this creed as follows: "Once, when I was reciting the *Quicúmque vult*, I was shown so clearly how it was possible for there to be One God alone and Three Persons, that it caused me both amazement and much comfort. It was of the greatest help in teaching me to know more of the greatness of God and of his marvels."[3]

Ant. Glory be to you, equal Trinity, one Godhead, before all time, now and for ever. (Easter Time Alleluia.)

1. Whoever wishes to be saved must, above all, keep the Catholic faith.

2. For unless a person keeps this faith whole and entire, he will undoubtedly be lost for ever.

3. This is what the Catholic faith teaches: we worship one God in the Trinity and the Trinity in unity.

4. We distinguish among the Persons, but we do not divide the substance.

5. For the Father is a distinct Person; the Son is a distinct Person; and the Holy Spirit is a distinct Person.

6. Still, the Father and the Son and the Holy Spirit have one divinity, equal glory, and coeternal majesty.

7. What the Father is, the Son is, and the Holy Spirit is.

8. The Father is uncreated, the Son is uncreated, and the Holy Spirit is uncreated.

9. The Father is boundless, the Son is boundless, and the Holy Spirit is boundless.

10. The Father is eternal, the Son is eternal, and the Holy Spirit is eternal.

11. Nevertheless, there are not three eternal beings, but one eternal being.

12. Thus there are not three uncreated beings, nor three boundless beings, but one uncreated being and one boundless being.

3. *Life of St. Teresa of Jesus* 39.36.

13. Likewise, the Father is omnipotent, the Son is omnipotent, and the Holy Spirit is omnipotent.

14. Yet there are not three omnipotent beings, but one omnipotent being.

15. Thus the Father is God, the Son is God, and the Holy Spirit is God.

16. But there are not three gods, but one God.

17. The Father is Lord, the Son is Lord, and the Holy Spirit is Lord.

18. There are not three lords, but one Lord.

19. For according to Christian truth, we must profess that each of the Persons individually is God; and according to Christian religion, we are forbidden to say that there are three gods or three lords.

20. The Father is not made by anyone, nor created by anyone, nor generated by anyone.

21. The Son is not made nor created, but is generated by the Father alone.

22. The Holy Spirit is not made nor created nor generated, but proceeds from the Father and the Son.

23. There is, then, one Father, not three fathers; one Son, not three sons; one Holy Spirit, not three holy spirits.

24. In this Trinity, there is nothing greater, nothing less than anything else, but all three Persons are coeternal and coequal with one another.

25. So that, as we have said, we worship complete unity in the Trinity and the Trinity in unity.

26. This, then, is what one who wishes to be saved must believe about the Trinity.

27. It is also necessary for eternal salvation that one believe steadfastly in the incarnation of our Lord Jesus Christ.

28. The true faith is: we believe and profess that our Lord Jesus Christ, the Son of God, is both God and man.

29. As God, he was begotten of the substance of the Father before time; as man, he was born in time of the substance of his Mother.

30. He is perfect God; and he is perfect man, with a rational soul and human flesh.

31. He is equal to the Father in his divinity, but he is inferior to the Father in his humanity.

32. Although he is God and man, he is not two, but one Christ.

33. And he is one, not because his divinity was changed into flesh, but because his humanity was assumed to God.

34. He is one, not at all because of a mingling of substances, but because he is one person.

35. As a rational soul and flesh are one man: so God and man are one Christ.

36. He died for our salvation, descended to hell, arose from the dead on the third day,

37. Ascended into heaven, sits at the right hand of God the Father almighty, and from there he shall come to judge the living and the dead.

38. At his coming, all are to arise with their own bodies; and they are to give an account of their lives.

39. Those who have done good deeds will go into eternal life; those who have done evil will go into everlasting fire.

40. This is the Catholic faith. Everyone must believe it, firmly and steadfastly; otherwise, one cannot be saved.

Glory be…

Ant. Glory be to you, coequal Trinity, one Godhead, before all time, now and for ever. (Easter Time Alleluia.)

℣. O Lord, hear my prayer.

℟. **And let my cry come unto you.**

Priests add:

℣. The Lord be with you.

℟. **And with your spirit.**

Let us pray.

Almighty, ever-living God, who have permitted us, your servants, in our profession of the true faith, to acknowledge the glory of the eternal Trinity, and in the power of that majesty to adore the Unity, grant that, by steadfastness in this same faith, we may be ever guarded against all adversity. We ask this through our Lord Jesus Christ, your Son, who lives and reigns with you and the Holy Spirit, one God, for ever and ever.

℟. **Amen.**

ANGELIC TRISAGION

The Holy Trinity is the central mystery of our faith. The feast of the Holy Trinity is celebrated on the Sunday after Pentecost. The Angelic Trisagion is said for the three days beginning on the Friday prior to Trinity Sunday.

In the name of the Father, and of the Son, and of the Holy Spirit. Amen.

℣. Lord, open my lips.

℟. **And my mouth shall declare your praise.**

℣. O God, come to my assistance.

℟. **O Lord, make haste to help me.**

℣. Glory be…

℟. **As it was…**

Decades

All say the invocation, **Holy is God…**; afterwards, the Lord's Prayer is said as usual, with the priest (or whoever presides) answered by the people. Then, nine times whoever presides says the prayer **To You, O Blessed Trinity…** Each time, the people answer with the prayer **Holy, holy…** After the last repetition, the **Glory be…** is said.

Holy is God! Holy and strong! Holy Immortal One, have mercy on us. Our Father…

℣. To you, O Blessed Trinity, be praise and honor and thanksgiving, for ever and ever!

℟. **Holy, holy, holy Lord, God of hosts. Heaven and earth are filled with your glory.**

℣. Glory be…

℞. **As it was…**

The second and third decades are said in the same way, beginning with the words: **Holy is God…**

Ant. God the Father unbegotten, Only-Begotten Son, and Holy Spirit, the Comforter: holy and undivided Trinity, with all our hearts we acknowledge you: Glory to you for ever.

℣. Let us bless the Father and the Son with the Holy Spirit.

℞. **Be praised and exalted above all things for ever.**

Let us pray.

Almighty, ever-living God, who have permitted us, your servants, in our profession of the true Faith, to acknowledge the glory of the eternal Trinity, and in the power of that majesty to adore the Unity, grant that, by steadfastness in this same Faith, we may be ever guarded against all adversity. Through Christ our Lord.

℞. **Amen. Set us free, save us, vivify us, O Blessed Trinity!**

DEVOTIONS TO
OUR LORD JESUS CHRIST

Jesus Christ, having entered the sanctuary of heaven once and for all, intercedes constantly for us as the mediator who assures us of the permanent outpouring of the Holy Spirit.... There is no other way of Christian prayer but Christ.[1]

FIRST FRIDAY DEVOTION

The prayer of the Church venerates and honors the *Heart of Jesus*... which, out of love for men, he allowed to be pierced by our sins.[2]

Although devotion to the Sacred Heart of Jesus dates to before her time, it was St. Margaret Mary Alacoque who made it widespread. In 1675, within the octave of the feast of Corpus Christi, our Lord appeared to her and said: "Behold this heart which has so loved men that it spared nothing, even exhaust and consume itself, to prove to them its love. I receive from the greater part of men nothing but ingratitude, by the contempt, irreverence, sacrileges, and coldness with which they treat me in this sacrament of love [the Eucharist]. But what is still more painful to me is that even souls consecrated to me are acting in this way."[3]

I promise you in the excess of the mercy of my heart, that its all-powerful love will grant those who receive Communion on the first Friday of nine consecutive months the grace of final repentance; they shall not die under my displeasure, nor without receiving the Last Sacraments; my divine mercy shall be their assured refuge at that last hour.[4]

The great promise of the Sacred Heart is most consoling: the grace of final perseverance and the joy of having Jesus' heart as our sure refuge and infinite ocean of mercy in our last hour.

---

1. CCC 667, 2664.
2. CCC 2669.
3. *St. Margaret M. Alacoque*, Autobiography.
4. Ibid.

To gain this grace, we must:

* Receive holy Communion on nine consecutive first Fridays.

* Have the intention of honoring the Sacred Heart of Jesus and of reaching final perseverance.

* Offer each Holy Communion as an act of atonement for offenses against the Blessed Sacrament.

Introductory Prayer

Almighty and everlasting God, look upon the heart of your well-beloved Son and upon the praise and satisfaction which he offers to you in the name of all sinners; and grant them pardon when they seek your mercy. We ask this in the name of Jesus Christ, your Son, who lives and reigns with you for ever and ever.

℟. **Amen.**

Reading   Jn 19: 31-37

Since it was the day of Preparation, in order to prevent the bodies from remaining on the cross on the Sabbath (for that Sabbath was a high day), the Jews asked Pilate that their legs might be broken, and that they might be taken away. So the soldiers came and broke the legs of the first, and of the other who had been crucified with him; but when they came to Jesus and saw that he was already dead, they did not break his legs. But one of the soldiers pierced his side with a spear, and at once there came out blood and water.

He who saw it has borne witness—his testimony is true, and he knows that he tells the truth—that you also may believe. For these things took place that the scripture might be fulfilled, "Not a bone of him shall be broken." And again another scripture says, "They shall look on him whom they have pierced."

Considerations[5]

1. Love is revealed to us in the Incarnation, the redemptive journey which Jesus Christ made on our earth, culminating in the supreme sacrifice of the cross. And on the cross it showed itself through a new sign: "One of the soldiers pierced his side with a spear, and at once there came out blood and water." This water and blood of Jesus speak to us of a self-sacrifice brought to the last extreme: "It is finished"—everything is achieved, for the sake of love....

The fullness of God is revealed and given to us in Christ, in the love of Christ, in Christ's heart. For it is the heart of him in whom "the whole fullness of deity dwells bodily." Were one to lose sight of this great plan of God—the overflow of love in the world through the Incarnation, the Redemption, and Pentecost—he could not understand the refinement with which our Lord deals with us.

2. Let us realize all the richness hidden in the words "the Sacred Heart of Jesus." When we speak of a person's heart, we refer not just to his sentiments, but to the whole person in his loving dealings with others. In order to help us understand divine things, Scripture uses the expression "heart" in its full human meaning, as the summary and source, expression and ultimate basis, of one's thoughts, words, and actions. One is worth what one's heart is worth....

So, when we talk about the heart of Jesus, we stress the certainty of God's love and the truth of his commitment to us. When we recommend devotion to the Sacred Heart, we are recommending that we should give our whole selves to Jesus, to the whole Jesus—our souls, our feelings and thoughts, our words and actions, our joys.

That is what true devotion to the heart of Jesus means. It is knowing God and ourselves. It is looking at Jesus and turning to him, letting him encourage and teach and guide us. The only difficulty that could beset this devotion would be our own failure to understand the reality of an incarnate God.

---

5. This section comes from St. Josemaria Escriva's *Finding Peace in the Heart of Christ* (Princeton, N.J: Scepter Publishers, 1974), 162-170. Footnotes used by the author in the original homily are omitted.

3. Jesus on the cross, with his heart overflowing with love for us, is such an eloquent commentary on the value of people and things that words only get in the way. Men, their happiness and their lives, are so important that the very Son of God gave himself to redeem and cleanse and raise them up. "Who will not love this heart so wounded?" a contemplative asks in this connection. "Who will not return love for love? Who will not embrace a heart so pure? We, who are made of flesh, will repay love with love. We will embrace our wounded One, whose hands and feet ungodly men have nailed; we will cling to his side and to his heart. Let us pray that we be worthy of linking our heart with his love and of wounding it with a lance, for it is still hard and impenitent...."

But note that God does not say: "In exchange for your own heart, I will give you a will of pure spirit." No, he gives us a heart, a human heart, like Christ's. I don't have one heart for loving God and another for loving people. I love Christ and the Father and the Holy Spirit and our Lady with the same heart with which I love my parents and my friends. I shall never tire of repeating this. We must be very human, for otherwise we cannot be divine....

If we don't learn from Jesus, we will never love. If, like some people, we were to think that to keep a clean heart, a heart worthy of God, means "not mixing it up, not contaminating it" with human affection, we would become insensitive to other people's pain and sorrow. We would be capable of only an "official charity," something dry and soulless. But ours would not be the true charity of Jesus Christ, which involves affection and human warmth. In saying this, I am not supporting the mistaken theories—pitiful excuses—that misdirect hearts away from God and lead them into occasions of sin and perdition....

4. But I have still a further consideration to put before you. We have to fight vigorously to do good, precisely because it is difficult for us to resolve seriously to be just, and there is a long way to go before human relations are inspired by love and not hatred or indifference. We should also be aware that, even if we achieve a reasonable distribution of wealth and a harmonious organization of society, there will

still be the suffering of illness, of misunderstanding, of loneliness, of the death of loved ones, of the experience of our own limitations.

Faced with the weight of all this, a Christian can find only one genuine answer, a definitive answer: Christ on the cross, a God who suffers and dies, a God who gives us his heart opened by a lance for the love of us all. Our Lord abominates injustice and condemns those who commit it. But he respects the freedom of each individual. He permits injustice to happen because, as a result of original sin, it is part and parcel of the human condition. Yet his heart is full of love for men. Our suffering, our sadness, our anguish, our hunger and thirst for justice . . . he took all these tortures on himself by means of the cross. . . .

Suffering is part of God's plans. This is the truth, however difficult it may be for us to understand it. It was difficult for Jesus Christ the man to undergo his passion: "Father, if you are willing, remove this cup from me; nevertheless, not my will, but yours, be done." In this tension of pleading and acceptance of the Father's will, Jesus goes calmly to his death, pardoning those who crucify him.

This supernatural acceptance of suffering was, precisely, the greatest of all conquests. By dying on the cross, Jesus overcame death. God brings life from death. The attitude of a child of God is not one of resignation to a possibly tragic fate; it is the sense of achievement of someone who has a foretaste of victory. In the name of this victorious love of Christ, we Christians should go out into the world to be sowers of peace and joy through everything we say and do. We have to fight—a fight of peace—against evil, against injustice, against sin. Thus do we serve notice that the present condition of mankind is not definitive. *Only* the love of God, shown in the heart of Christ, will attain our glorious spiritual triumph.

CONSECRATION TO THE SACRED HEART OF JESUS

St. Margaret Mary Alacoque

"The prayer of the Church venerates and honors the *Heart of Jesus* just as it invokes his most holy name. It adores the incarnate Word and his Heart which, out of love for men, he allowed to be pierced by our sins. Christian prayer loves to follow the way of the cross in the Savior's steps" (CCC 2669).

To the Sacred Heart of our Lord Jesus Christ, I give myself, and I consecrate my person and my life, my actions, pains, and sufferings, so that I may be unwilling to make use of any part of my being other than to honor, love, and glorify the Sacred Heart.

This is my unchanging purpose, namely, to be all his and to do all things for the love of him, at the same time renouncing with all my heart whatever is displeasing to him. I therefore take you, O Sacred Heart, to be the only object of my love, the guardian of my life, my assurance of salvation, the remedy of my weakness and inconstancy, the atonement for all the faults of my life, and my sure refuge at the hour of death.

Be, then, O Heart of goodness, my justification before God the Father, and turn away from me the strokes of his righteous anger. O Heart of love, I put all my confidence in you, for I fear everything from my own wickedness and frailty, but I hope for all things from your goodness and bounty.

Remove from me all that can displease you or resist your holy will; let your pure love imprint your image so deeply upon my heart that I shall never be able to forget you or to be separated from you.

May I obtain from your loving kindness the grace of having my name written in your heart, for in you I desire to place all my happiness and glory, living and dying in bondage to you.

Concluding Prayer

Father, we honor the heart of your Son, broken by our cruelty, yet symbol of love's triumph, pledge of all that we are called to be. Teach us to see Christ in the lives we touch and to offer him living worship by love-filled service to our brothers and sisters.

We ask this through Christ our Lord.

LITANY OF THE SACRED HEART OF JESUS

According to tradition, this litany, approved in 1899 for public recitation, originated at Marseilles, where devotion to the Sacred Heart became very popular during the early eighteenth century.

Lord, have mercy on us **Christ, have mercy on us.**

Lord, have mercy on us.

   Christ, hear us. **Christ, graciously hear us.**

                                                 Have mercy on us.

God our Father in heaven

God the Son, Redeemer of the world…

God the Holy Spirit…

Holy Trinity, one God…

Heart of Jesus, Son of the eternal Father…

Heart of Jesus, formed by the Holy Spirit
   in the womb of the Virgin Mother…

Heart of Jesus, one with the eternal Word…

Heart of Jesus, infinite in majesty…

Heart of Jesus, holy temple of God…

Heart of Jesus, tabernacle of the Most High…

Heart of Jesus, house of God and gate of heaven…

Heart of Jesus, aflame with love for us…

Heart of Jesus, source of justice and love…

Heart of Jesus, full of goodness and love…

Heart of Jesus, wellspring of all virtue…

Heart of Jesus, worthy of all praise…

Heart of Jesus, king and center of all hearts…

Heart of Jesus, treasure-house of wisdom and knowledge…

Heart of Jesus, in whom there dwells the fullness of God…

Heart of Jesus, in whom the Father is well pleased…

Heart of Jesus, from whose fullness we have all received…

Heart of Jesus, desire of the eternal hills…

Heart of Jesus, patient and full of mercy…

Heart of Jesus, generous to all who turn to you…

Heart of Jesus, fountain of life and holiness…

Heart of Jesus, atonement for our sins ,   **Have mercy on us.**
Heart of Jesus, overwhelmed with insults…
Heart of Jesus, broken for our sins…
Heart of Jesus, obedient even to death…
Heart of Jesus, pierced by a lance…
Heart of Jesus, source of all consolation…
Heart of Jesus, our life and resurrection…
Heart of Jesus, our peace and reconciliation…
Heart of Jesus, victim for our sins…
Heart of Jesus, salvation of all who trust in you…
Heart of Jesus, hope of all who die in you…
Heart of Jesus, delight of all the saints…

Lamb of God, who take away
      the sins of the world,   **Spare us, O Lord.**
Lamb of God, who take away
      the sins of the world,   **Graciously hear us, O Lord.**
Lamb of God, who take away
      the sins of the world,   **Have mercy on us.**

℣. Jesus, gentle and humble of heart,

℟. **Touch our hearts and make them like your own.**

Let us pray.

Father,
we rejoice in the gifts of love
we have received from the heart of Jesus, your Son.
Open our hearts to share his life
and continue to bless us with his love.
We ask this in the name of Jesus the Lord.

℟. **Amen.**

STATIONS OF THE CROSS

As Christians we should love to follow the Way of the Cross in the Savior's footsteps. The Stations, from the Prætorium to Golgotha and the tomb, trace the Passion and Death of Christ, who by his Holy Cross has redeemed the world. To understand the mystery of Redemption and the *salvific meaning of suffering*, one ought to meditate upon the sufferings of our Lord, which he took upon himself to save us from sin. God is always with those who suffer. His omnipotence is manifested precisely in the fact that he freely accepted suffering. He could have chosen not to do so. He could have chosen to demonstrate his omnipotence even at the moment of the Crucifixion.[6]

In the name of the Father, and of the Son,
and of the Holy Spirit. Amen.

My Lord and my God,
under the loving eyes of our Mother,
we are making ready to accompany you
along this path of sorrow
which was the price paid for our redemption.
We wish to suffer all that you suffered,
to offer you our poor, contrite hearts,
because you are innocent, and yet
you are going to die for us,
who are the only really guilty ones.
My mother, Virgin of sorrows,
help us to relive those bitter hours
which your Son wished to spend on earth,
so that we, who were made from a handful of clay,
may finally live
in libertátem glóriæ filiórum Dei,
in the freedom and glory of the children of God.

---

6. For more on this great mystery, cf. St. John Paul II, *Salvifici Doloris* [On the Christian Meaning of Suffering] 14. The remainder of this section is a reprint from St. Josemaria Escriva, *The Way of the Cross*.

FIRST STATION

JESUS IS CONDEMNED TO DEATH

℣. We adore you, O Christ, and we bless you.

℟. **Because, by your holy cross, you have redeemed the world.**

It is after ten in the morning. The trial is moving to its close. There has been no conclusive evidence. The judge knows that his enemies have handed Jesus over to him out of envy, and he tries an absurd move: a choice between Barabbas, a criminal accused of robbery and murder, and Jesus, who says he is Christ. The people choose Barrabas, and Pilate exclaims: *What am I to do, then, with Jesus?* (Mt 27: 22).

They all reply: *Crucify him!* The judge insists: *Why, what evil has he done?* Once again they respond, shouting: *Crucify him! Crucify him!*

Pilate is frightened by the growing uproar. So he sends for water and washes his hands in the sight of the people, saying as he does so: *I am innocent of the blood of this just man; it is your affair* (Mt 27: 24).

And having had Jesus scourged, he hands him over to them to be crucified. Their frenzied and possessed throats fall silent, as if God had already been vanquished.

* Jesus is all alone. Far off now are the days when the words of the Man-God brought light and hope to men's hearts, those long processions of sick people whom he healed, the triumphant acclaim of Jerusalem when the Lord arrived, riding on a gentle donkey. If only men had wanted to give a different outlet for God's love! If only you and I had recognized the day of the Lord!

---

* You may wish to kneel here.

SECOND STATION

JESUS TAKES UP HIS CROSS

℣. We adore you, O Christ, and we bless you.

℞. **Because, by your holy cross, you have redeemed the world.**

Outside the city, to the northwest of Jerusalem, there is a little hill: Golgotha is its name in Aramaic; *locus Calvariæ*, in Latin: the place of skulls, or Calvary.

Offering no resistance, Jesus gives himself up to the execution of the sentence. He is to be spared nothing, and upon his shoulders falls the weight of the ignominious cross. But, through love, the cross is to become the throne from which he reigns.

The people of Jerusalem and those from abroad who have come for the Passover push their way through the city streets, to catch a passing glimpse of Jesus of Nazareth, the King of the Jews. There is a tumult of voices, and, now and then, short silences — perhaps when Jesus fixes his eyes on someone:

If anyone wishes to come after me, let him take up his cross daily and follow me (Mt 16: 24).

How lovingly Jesus embraces the wood which is to bring him to death!

* Is it not true that as soon as you cease to be afraid of the cross, of what people call the cross, when you set your will to accept the will of God, then you find happiness, and all your worries, all your sufferings, physical or moral, pass away?

Truly the cross of Jesus is gentle and lovable. There, sorrows cease to count; there is only the joy of knowing that we are coredeemers with him.

THIRD STATION

JESUS FALLS THE FIRST TIME

℣. We adore you, O Christ, and we bless you.

℞. **Because, by your holy cross, you have redeemed the world.**

The heavy cross cuts and tears into our Lord's shoulders.

The crowd has swollen into a multitude, and the legionaries can scarcely contain the angry, surging mob which, like a river that has burst its banks, flows through the streets and alleyways of Jerusalem.

The worn-out body of Jesus staggers now beneath the huge cross. His most loving heart can barely summon up another breath of life for his poor wounded limbs.

To his right and left, our Lord sees the multitude moving around like sheep without a shepherd. He could call them one by one by their names—by our names. There they are, those who were fed at the multiplication of the loaves and fishes, those who were cured of their ailments, those he taught by the lakeside, on the mountain, and in the porticoes of the Temple.

A sharp pain pierces the soul of Jesus; our Lord falls to the ground, exhausted.

 * You and I can say nothing: now we know why the cross of Jesus weighs so much. We weep over our wretched failings and also for the terrible ingratitude of the human heart. From the depths of our soul there comes an act of real contrition, which lifts us up from the prostration of sin. Jesus has fallen that we might get up: once and for all.

FOURTH STATION

JESUS MEETS HIS BLESSED MOTHER

℣. We adore you, O Christ, and we bless you.

℞. **Because, by your holy cross, you have redeemed the world.**

No sooner has Jesus risen from his first fall than he meets his Blessed Mother, standing by the wayside where he is passing.

With immense love Mary looks at Jesus, and Jesus at his mother. Their eyes meet, and each heart pours into the other its own deep sorrow. Mary's soul is steeped in bitter grief, the grief of Jesus Christ.

O all you that pass by the way, look and see, was there ever a sorrow to compare with my sorrow! (Lam 1: 12).

But no one notices, no one pays attention; only Jesus.

Simeon's prophecy has been fulfilled: *Thine own soul a sword shall pierce* (Lk 2:35).

In the dark loneliness of the Passion, our Lady offers her son a comforting balm of tenderness, of union, of faithfulness; a "yes" to the divine will.

* Hand in hand with Mary, you and I also want to console Jesus, by accepting always and in everything the will of his Father, of our Father.

Only thus will we taste the sweetness of Christ's cross and come to embrace it with all the strength of Love, carrying it in triumph along the ways of the earth

FIFTH STATION

SIMON OF CYRENE HELPS JESUS TO CARRY THE CROSS

℣. We adore you, O Christ, and we bless you.

℟. **Because, by your holy cross, you have redeemed the world.**

Jesus is exhausted. His footsteps become more and more unsteady, and the soldiers are in a hurry to be finished. So when they are going out of the city through the Judgment Gate, they take hold of a man who is coming in from a farm, a man called Simon of Cyrene, the father of Alexander and Rufus, and they force him to carry the cross of Jesus (cf. Mk 15: 21).

In the whole context of the Passion, this help does not add up to very much. But, for Jesus, a smile, a word, a gesture or a little bit of love is enough for him to pour out his grace bountifully on the soul of his friend. Years later, Simon's sons, Christians by then, will be known and held in high esteem among their brothers in the faith. And it all started with this unexpected meeting with the cross.

I went to those who were not looking for me; I was found by those that sought me not (Is 65: 1).

* At times the cross appears without our looking for it: It is Christ who is seeking *us* out. And if by chance, before this unexpected cross which, perhaps, is therefore more difficult to understand, your heart were to show repugnance . . . don't give it consolations. And, filled with a noble compassion, when it asks for them, say to it slowly, as one speaking in confidence: "Heart: heart on the cross! Heart on the cross!"

SIXTH STATION

VERONICA WIPES THE FACE OF JESUS

℣. We adore you, O Christ, and we bless you.

℟. **Because, by your holy cross, you have redeemed the world.**

There is no beauty in him, nor comeliness: and we have seen him and there was no sightliness, that we should be attracted to him. Despised and the most abject of men, a man of sorrows and acquainted with infirmity; and his look was, as it were, hidden and despised. Whereupon we esteemed him not (cf. Is 53: 2-3).

It is the Son of God who is passing by, a madman… madly in love!

A woman, Veronica by name, makes her way through the crowd, with a white linen cloth folded in her hands, and with this she reverently wipes the face of Jesus. Our Lord leaves the impression of his holy Face on the three parts of the veil.

The beloved face of Jesus, which had smiled upon children and was transfigured with glory on Mount Tabor, is now, as it were, concealed by suffering. But this suffering is our purification; the sweat and the blood which disfigure and tarnish his features, serve to cleanse us.

  * Lord, help me to decide to tear off, through penance, this pitiful mask that I have fashioned with my wretched doings…. Then, and only then, by following the path of contemplation and atonement, will my life begin to copy faithfully the features of your life. I will find myself becoming more and more like you.

We will be other christs, Christ himself, *ipse Christus*.

SEVENTH STATION

JESUS FALLS A SECOND TIME

℣. We adore you, O Christ, and we bless you.

℞. **Because, by your holy cross, you have redeemed the world.**

Outside the walls of the city, the body of Jesus again gives way through weakness, and he falls a second time, amid the shouts of the crowd and the rough handling of the soldiers.

Infirmity of body and bitterness of soul have caused Jesus to fall again. All the sins of men — mine too — weigh down on his Sacred Humanity.

He has borne our infirmities and carried our sorrows, and we have taken him for a leper, and as one struck by God and afflicted. But he was wounded for our iniquities and bruised for our sins. On him fell the punishment that brought us salvation, and by his wounds we have been healed (Is 53: 4-5).

Jesus stumbles, but his fall lifts us up; his death brings us back to life.

To our falling again and again into evil, Jesus responds with his determination to redeem us, with an abundance of forgiveness. And, so that no one may despair, again he wearily raises himself, embracing the cross.

* May our stumbles and defeats separate us from him no more. Just as a feeble child throws himself contritely into the strong arms of his father, you and I will hold tightly to the yoke of Jesus. Only a contrition and humility like this can transform our human weakness into the fortitude of God.

EIGHTH STATION

JESUS CONSOLES
THE WOMEN OF JERUSALEM

℣. We adore you, O Christ, and we bless you.

℟. **Because, by your holy cross, you have redeemed the world.**

Among the people watching our Lord as he passes by are a number of women who, unable to restrain their compassion, break into tears, perhaps recalling those glorious days spent with Jesus, when everyone exclaimed in amazement: *Bene ómnia fecit* ("He has done all things well"—Mk 7: 37).

But our Lord wishes to channel their weeping towards a more supernatural motive. He invites them to weep for sins, which are the cause of the Passion and which will draw down the rigor of divine justice:

Daughters of Jerusalem, weep not for me, but for yourselves and for your children. . . . For if they do these things to the green wood, what shall be done to the dry? (Lk 23: 28, 31).

 * Your sins, my sins, the sins of all men, rise up. All the evil we have done and the good that we have neglected to do. The desolate panorama of the countless crimes and iniquities which we would have committed, if he, Jesus, had not strengthened us with the light of his most loving glance.

How little a life is for making atonement!

NINTH STATION

JESUS FALLS THE THIRD TIME

℣. We adore you, O Christ, and we bless you.

℟. **Because, by your holy cross, you have redeemed the world.**

Our Lord falls for the third time, on the slope leading up to Calvary, with only forty or fifty paces between him and the summit. Jesus can no longer stay on his feet: his strength has failed him, and he lies on the ground in utter exhaustion.

He offered himself up because it was his will; abused and ill-treated, he opened not his mouth, as a sheep led to the slaughter, dumb as a lamb before its shearers (Is 53: 7).

Everyone against him . . . the people of the city and those from abroad, and the Pharisees and the soldiers and the chief priests.... All of them executioners. His mother—my mother—weeps.

Jesus fulfills the will of his Father! Poor; naked. Generous: what is there left for him to surrender? *Diléxit me, et trádidit semetípsum pro me* ("He loved me and delivered himself up unto death for me—Gal 2: 20).

	*	My God! May I hate sin and unite myself to you, taking the holy cross into my arms, so that I, in my turn, may fulfill your most lovable will... stripped of every earthly attachment, with no other goal but your glory... generously, not keeping anything back, offering myself with you in a perfect holocaust.

TENTH STATION

JESUS IS STRIPPED OF HIS GARMENTS

℣. We adore you, O Christ, and we bless you.

℟. **Because, by your holy cross, you have redeemed the world.**

When our Lord arrives at Calvary, he is given some wine to drink mixed with gall, as a narcotic to lessen in some way the pain of the crucifixion. But Jesus, after tasting it to show his gratitude for that kind service, has not wanted to drink (cf. Mt 27: 34). He gives himself up to death with the full freedom of love.

Then the soldiers strip Christ of his garments.

From the soles of his feet to the top of his head, there is nothing healthy in him: wounds and bruises and swelling sores. They are not bound up, nor dressed, nor anointed with oil (Is 1: 6).

The executioners take his garments and divide them into four parts. But the cloak is without seam, so they say:

It would be better not to tear it, but let us cast lots for it to see whose it shall be (Jn 19: 24).

Thus, Scripture is again fulfilled: *They divided my garments among them, and upon my vesture they cast lots* (Ps 22: 19).

* Despoiled, stripped, left in the most absolute poverty, our Lord is left with nothing, save the wood of the cross.

For us to reach God, Christ is the way; but Christ is on the cross, and to climb up to the cross we must have our heart free, not tied to earthly things.

ELEVENTH STATION

JESUS IS NAILED TO THE CROSS

℣. We adore you, O Christ, and we bless you.

℟. **Because, by your holy cross, you have redeemed the world.**

Now they are crucifying our Lord, and with him two thieves, one on his right and one on his left. Meanwhile, Jesus says:

Father, forgive them, for they do not know what they are doing (Lk 23: 34).

It is Love that has brought Jesus to Calvary. And, on the cross, all his gestures, all his words are of love, a love both calm and strong.

With a gesture befitting an eternal priest without father or mother, without lineage (cf. Heb 7: 3), he opens his arms to the whole human race.

With the hammerblows with which Jesus is being nailed, there resound the prophetic words of holy Scripture: *They have pierced my hands and feet; I can count all my bones. They stare and gloat over me* (Ps 22: 17-18).

My people, what have I done to thee, or in what have I saddened thee? Answer me! (Mi 6: 3).

* And we, our souls rent with sorrow, say to Jesus in all sincerity: I am yours, and I give my whole self to you; gladly I accept being nailed myself to your cross, ready to be in the crossroads of this world a soul dedicated to you, to your glory, to the work of Redemption, the coredemption of the whole human race.

TWELFTH STATION

JESUS DIES ON THE CROSS

℣. We adore you, O Christ, and we bless you.

℞. **Because, by your holy cross, you have redeemed the world.**

On the uppermost part of the cross, the reason for the sentence is written: *Jesus of Nazareth, King of the Jews* (Jn 19: 19). And all who pass by insult him and jeer at him. *If he is the king of Israel, let him come down here and now from the cross* (Mt 27: 42).

One of the thieves comes to his defense: *This man has done no evil…* (Lk 23: 41). Then, turning to Jesus, he makes a humble request, full of faith: *Lord, remember me when thou comest into thy kingdom* (Lk 23: 42).

Truly, I say to thee: This day thou shalt be with me in Paradise (Lk 23: 43).

At the foot of the cross stands his mother, Mary, with other holy women. Jesus looks at her; then he looks at the disciple whom he loves, and he says to his mother: *Woman, behold thy son.* Then he says to the disciple: *Behold thy mother* (Jn 19: 26-27).

The sun's light is extinguished, and the earth is left in darkness. It is close to three o'clock, when Jesus cries out: *Eli, Eli, lamma sabacthani? That is: My God, my God, why hast thou forsaken me?* (Mt 27: 46).

Then, knowing that all things are about to be accomplished, that the scriptures may be fulfilled, he says: *I am thirsty* (Jn 19: 28). The soldiers soak a sponge in vinegar and, placing it on a reed of hyssop, put it to his mouth. Jesus sips the vinegar, and exclaims: *It is accomplished!* (Jn 19: 29-30).

The veil of the temple is rent, and the earth trembles, when the Lord cries out in a loud voice: *Father, into thy hands I commend my spirit* (Mt 27: 51; Lk 23: 45-46). And he expires.

    * Love sacrifice; it is a fountain of interior life. Love the cross, which is an altar of sacrifice. Love pain, until you drink, as Christ did, the very dregs of the chalice.

THIRTEENTH STATION

JESUS IS LAID IN THE ARMS
OF HIS BLESSED MOTHER

℣. We adore you, O Christ, and we bless you.

℟. **Because, by your holy cross, you have redeemed the world.**

Mary stands by the cross, engulfed in grief. And John is beside her. But it is getting late, and the Jews press for our Lord to be removed from there.

Having obtained from Pilate the permission required by Roman law for the burial of condemned prisoners, there comes to Calvary *a councillor named Joseph, a good and upright man, a native of Arimathea. He has not consented to their counsel and their doings, but is himself one of those waiting for the kingdom of God* (cf. Lk 23: 50-51). With him, too, comes Nicodemus, *the same man who earlier visited Jesus by night; he brings with him a mixture of myrrh and aloes about a hundred pounds in weight* (cf. Jn 19: 39).

These men are not known publicly as disciples of the Master. They were not present at the great miracles, nor did they accompany him on his triumphal entry into Jerusalem. But now, when things have turned bad, when the others have fled, they are not afraid to stand up for their Lord.

Between the two of them they take down the body of Jesus and place it in the arms of his most holy mother. Mary's grief is renewed.

* *Where has thy Beloved gone, O fairest of women? Where has he whom thou lovest gone, and we will seek him with thee?* (Sg 6: 1). The Blessed Virgin is our mother, and we do not wish to—we cannot—leave her alone.

FOURTEENTH STATION

JESUS IS LAID IN THE TOMB

℣. We adore you, O Christ, and we bless you.

℟. **Because, by your holy cross, you have redeemed the world.**

Very near Calvary, in an orchard, Joseph of Arimathea had a new tomb made, cut out of the rock. Since it is the eve of the solemn Pasch of the Jews, Jesus is laid there. Then Joseph, *rolling a great stone, closes the grave door and goes away* (Mt 27: 60).

Jesus came into the world with nothing. So, too, with nothing—not even the place where he rests—he has left us.

The mother of our Lord—my mother—and the women who have followed the Master from Galilee, after taking careful note of everything, also take their leave. Night falls.

Now it is all over. The work of our redemption has been accomplished. We are now children of God, because Jesus has died for us and his death has ransomed us. *Empti enim estis prétio magno!* (1 Cor 6: 20). You and I have been bought at a great price.

* We must bring into our life, to make them our own, the life and death of Christ. We must die through mortification and penance, so that Christ may live in us through love. And then follow in the footsteps of Christ, with a zeal to coredeem all mankind.

We must give our life for others. That is the only way to live the life of Jesus Christ and to become one and the same thing with him.

ACCEPTANCE OF DEATH

We, too, O God, will descend into the grave whenever it shall please you, as it shall please you, and wheresoever it shall please you. Let your just decrees be fulfilled; let our sinful bodies return to their parent dust, but, in your great mercy, receive our immortal souls, and when our bodies have risen again, place them likewise in your kingdom, that we may love and bless you for ever and ever.

℟. **Amen**.

or:

Dear God and Father of mine, Lord of life and death, with an immutable decree you have established that, as a just chastisement for our sins, all of us have to die. Look at me here bent low before you. From the bottom of my heart, I abhor my past faults, for which I have merited death a thousand times, a death that I now accept as atonement for my sins and as proof of my submission to your lovable will. O Lord, happily will I die at the moment, in the place, and in the way that you want. And until that day I will take advantage of the days of life that remain in order to fight against my defects and grow in your love, to break the bonds that tie my heart to creatures, and to prepare my soul to appear in your presence; and from this moment on I abandon myself without reserve into the arms of your fatherly providence.

PRAYER OF ST. AUGUSTINE

Lord Jesus, let me know myself and know you, And desire nothing, save only you. Let me hate myself and love you. Let me do everything for the sake of you. Let me humble myself and exalt you. Let me think of nothing except you. Let me die to myself and live in you. Let me accept whatever happens as from you. Let me banish self and follow you, And ever desire to follow you. Let me fly from myself and take refuge in you, That I may deserve to be defended by you. Let me fear for myself, let me fear you, And let me be among those who are chosen by you. Let me distrust myself and put my trust in you. Let me be willing to obey for the sake of you. Let me cling to nothing, save only to you, And let me be poor because of you. Look upon me, that I may love you. Call me, that I may see you, And for ever enjoy you. Amen.

ACCEPTANCE OF DIVINE WILL

May the most just, the most lovable, and the most high Will of God be done, be fulfilled, be praised and exalted in all things forever. Amen.

PRAYER OF ST. ANDREW

The apostle Andrew was martyred by being nailed to a cross. His desire to be identified with Christ was so great that, when he was being led toward the place of his martyrdom and saw his own cross in the distance, he is said to have cried:

O good Cross, made beautiful by the body of the Lord: long have I desired you, ardently have I loved you, unceasingly have I sought you out; and now you are ready for my eager soul. Receive me from among men and restore me to my Master, so that he—who, by means of you, in dying redeemed me—may receive me. Amen.

SONNET TO OUR LORD ON THE CROSS

Anonymous

I am not moved to love you, O my God,
That I might hope in promised heaven to dwell;
Nor am I moved by fear of pain in hell
To turn from sin and follow where you trod.
You move me, Lord, broken beneath the rod,
Or stretched out on the cross, as nails compel
Your hand to twitch. It moves me that we sell,
To mockery and death, your precious blood.
It is, O Christ, your love which moves me so,
That my love rests not on a promised prize;
Nor holy fear on threat of endless woe;
It is not milk and honey, but the flow
Of blood from blessed wounds before my eyes,
That waters my buried soul and makes it grow.

DEVOTIONS TO
THE HOLY SPIRIT

The traditonal form of petition to the Holy Spirit is to invoke the Father through Christ our Lord to give us the Consoler Spirit. Jesus insists on this petition to be made in his name at the very moment when he promises the gift of the Spirit of Truth. But the simplest and most direct prayer is also traditional, "Come, Holy Spirit," and every liturgical tradition has developed it in antiphons and hymns.[1]

TEN-DAY DEVOTION TO THE HOLY SPIRIT

"The day before you begin the Ten-Day Devotion, which is the eve of the glorious Ascension of our divine Redeemer, you must prepare yourself by making a firm resolution to live an interior life and, once you have begun, never again abandon it. Do not ask yourself how much this is going to cost you; look at only how much it is worth. This has always been the case: What is worth a lot costs a lot. And what is the effort we put into knowing ourselves, when we compare it with the great benefits that we derive from it?"[2]

FIRST DAY

Introductory Prayer[3]

Come, O Holy Spirit! Enlighten my understanding in order that I may know your commands; strengthen my heart against the snares of the enemy; enkindle my will. I have heard your voice, and I do not want to harden my heart and resist, saying, "Later... tomorrow." *Nunc cœpi!* Right now! Lest there be no tomorrow for me.

---

1. CCC 2671; cf. Lk 11: 13; Jn 14: 17; 15: 26; 16: 13.
2. F. J. del Valle, *About the Holy Spirit*, Dublin: Four Court Press, 1981.
3. Prayer to the Holy Spirit composed by St. Josemaria Escriva. Cf. Postulation for the Cause of Canonization of Msgr. Josemaria Escriva: *Historical Registry of the Founder [of Opus Dei]*, 20172, p. 145.

O Spirit of truth and of wisdom, Spirit of understanding and of counsel, Spirit of joy and of peace! I want what you want, because you want it, as you want it, when you want it.

Consideration[4]

*Pentecost: the day when the Holy Spirit
came down upon the Lord's disciples*

Having just read in the Acts of the Apostles about Pentecost, the day when the Holy Spirit came down upon the Lord's disciples, we are conscious of being present at the great display of God's power with which the Church's life began to spread among all nations. The victory Christ achieved through his obedience, his offering of himself on the cross, and his resurrection — his triumph over death and sin — is revealed here in all its divine splendor.

The disciples, witnesses of the glory of the risen Christ, were filled with the strength of the Holy Spirit. Their minds and hearts were opened to a new light. They had followed Christ and accepted his teachings with faith, but they were not always able to fathom the full meaning of his words. The Spirit of truth, who was to teach them all things[5] had not yet come. They knew that Jesus alone could give them words of eternal life, and they were ready to follow him and to give their lives for him. But they were weak, and in the time of trial, they fled and left him alone.

On Pentecost, all that is a thing of the past. The Holy Spirit, who is the Spirit of strength, has made them firm, strong, daring. The word of the apostles resounds forcefully through the streets of Jerusalem.

The men and women who have come to the city from all parts of the world listen with amazement. "Parthians and Medes and Elamites, and inhabitants of Mesopotamia, Judea, and Cappadocia, Pontus and Asia, Phrygia and Pamphylia, Egypt and the parts of Libya about Cyrene, and visitors from Rome, Jews as well as proselytes, Cretans and Arabs, we have heard them speaking in our own languages of the wonderful works of God."[6] These wonders, which take place before their own

---

4. The homily "The Great Unknown," in *Christ Is Passing By*, by St. Josemaria Escriva, is reprinted here divided into ten "Considerations."

5. Cf. Jn 16: 12-13.

6. Acts 2: 9-11.

eyes, lead them to listen to the preaching of the apostles. The Holy Spirit himself, who is acting through our Lord's disciples, moves the hearts of their listeners and leads them to the faith.

St. Luke tells us that after St. Peter had spoken and proclaimed Christ's resurrection, many of those present came up to him and asked: "Brethren, what shall we do?" The apostle answered: "Repent and be baptized, every one of you, in the name of Jesus Christ, for the forgiveness of your sins; and you will receive the gift of the Holy Spirit." And, on that day, the sacred text tells us, about three thousand were added to the Church.[7]

The solemn coming of the Holy Spirit on Pentecost was not an isolated event. There is hardly a page in the Acts of the Apostles where we fail to read about him and the action by which he guides, directs, and enlivens the life and work of the early Christian community. It is he who inspires St. Peter's preaching, who strengthens the faith of the disciples, who confirms with his presence the calling of the Gentiles, who sends Saul and Barnabas to the distant lands where they will open new paths for the teachings of Jesus.[8] In a word, his presence and doctrine are everywhere.

Concluding Prayer

Holy and divine Spirit! Through the intercession of the Blessed Virgin Mary, your spouse, bring the fullness of your gifts into our hearts. Comforted and strengthened by you, may we live according to your will and may we die praising your infinite mercy. Through Christ our Lord. Amen.

SECOND DAY

Introductory Prayer

Come, O Holy Spirit! Enlighten my understanding in order that I may know your commands; strengthen my heart against the snares of the enemy; enkindle my will. I have heard your voice, and I do not want to harden my heart and resist, saying, "Later… tomorrow." *Nunc coepi!* Right now! Lest there be no tomorrow for me.

---

7. Cf. Acts 2: 37-41.
8. Cf. Acts 4: 8; 4: 31; 10: 44-47; 13: 2-4.

O Spirit of truth and of wisdom, Spirit of understanding and of counsel, Spirit of joy and of peace! I want what you want, because you want it, as you want it, when you want it.

Consideration

The Holy Spirit: present in the Church for all time

The profound reality which we see in the texts of holy Scripture is not a remembrance from the past, from some golden age of the Church which has since been buried in history. Despite the weaknesses and the sins of every one of us, it is the reality of today's Church and the Church of all time. "I will ask the Father," our Lord told his disciples, "and he will give you another Counselor to dwell with you for ever."[9] Jesus has kept his promise. He has risen from the dead, and, in union with the eternal Father, he sends us the Holy Spirit to sanctify us and to give us life.

The strength and the power of God light up the face of the earth. The Holy Spirit is present in the Church of Christ for all time, so that it may be, always and in everything, a sign raised up before all nations, announcing to all people the goodness and the love of God. In spite of our great limitations, we can look up to heaven with confidence and joy: God loves us and frees us from our sins. The presence and the action of the Holy Spirit in the Church are a foretaste of eternal happiness, of the joy and peace for which we are destined by God.

Like the men and women who came up to Peter on Pentecost, we too have been baptized. In Baptism, our Father God has taken possession of our lives, has made us share in the life of Christ, and has given us the Holy Spirit. Holy Scripture tells us that God has saved us "through the baptism of regeneration and renewal by the Holy Spirit; whom he has abundantly poured out upon us through Jesus Christ our Savior, in order that, justified by his grace, we may be heirs in hope to life everlasting."[10]

The experience of our weakness and of our failings, the painful realization of the smallness and meanness of some who call themselves Christians, the apparent failure or aimlessness of some works of apostolate—all these things, which bring home to us the reality of sin and

---

9. Cf. Jn 14: 16; Is 11: 12.
10. Ti 3: 5-7.

human limitation, can still be a trial of our faith. Temptation and doubt can lead us to ask: where are the strength and the power of God? When that happens, we have to react by practicing the virtue of hope with greater purity and forcefulness and striving to be more faithful.

Concluding Prayer

Holy and divine Spirit! Through the intercession of the Blessed Virgin Mary, your spouse, bring the fullness of your gifts into our hearts. Comforted and strengthened by you, may we live according to your will and may we die praising your infinite mercy. Through Christ our Lord. Amen.

THIRD DAY

Introductory Prayer

Come, O Holy Spirit! Enlighten my understanding in order that I may know your commands; strengthen my heart against the snares of the enemy; enkindle my will. I have heard your voice, and I do not want to harden my heart and resist, saying, "Later... tomorrow." *Nunc cœpi!* Right now! Lest there be no tomorrow for me.

O Spirit of truth and of wisdom, Spirit of understanding and of counsel, Spirit of joy and of peace! I want what you want, because you want it, as you want it, when you want it.

Consideration

The Church: the body of Christ, enlivened by the Holy Spirit

Let me tell you about an event of my own personal life, that happened many years ago. One day I was with a friend of mine, a man who had a good heart but who did not have faith. Pointing toward a globe, he said, "Look, from North to South, from East to West." "What do you want me to look at?" I asked. His answer was: "The failure of Christ. For twenty centuries people have been trying to bring his doctrine to men's lives, and look at the result." I was filled with sadness. It is painful to realize that many people still don't know our Lord, and that among those who do know him, many live as though they did not. But that feeling lasted only a moment. It was shortly overcome by love and thankfulness, because Jesus has wanted every man to cooperate freely in the work of redemption. *He has not failed.* His doctrine and life have been effective in the world at all times. The redemption carried out by him is sufficient, and more than sufficient.

God does not want slaves, but children. *He respects our freedom.* The work of salvation is still going on, and each one of us has a part in it. It is Christ's will, St. Paul tells us in impressive words, that we should fulfill — in our flesh, in our life — that which is lacking in his Passion, "for the good of his body, which is the Church."[11]

It is worthwhile to put our lives on the line, to give ourselves completely, so as to answer to the love and the confidence that God has placed in us. It is worthwhile, above all, to decide to take our Christian life seriously. When we recite the Creed, we state that we believe in God the Father Almighty, in his Son Jesus Christ, who died and rose again, and in the Holy Spirit, the Lord and giver of life. We affirm that the Church — one, holy, catholic, and apostolic — is the body of Christ, enlivened by the Holy Spirit. We rejoice in the forgiveness of sins and in the hope of our own resurrection. But do those words penetrate to the depths of our own heart? Or do they remain only on our lips? The divine message of victory, the joy and the peace of Pentecost, should be the unshakable foundation for every Christian's way of thinking and acting and living.

Concluding Prayer

Holy and divine Spirit! Through the intercession of the Blessed Virgin Mary, your spouse, bring the fullness of your gifts into our hearts. Comforted and strengthened by you, may we live according to your will and may we die praising your infinite mercy. Through Christ our Lord. Amen.

FOURTH DAY

Introductory Prayer

Come, O Holy Spirit! Enlighten my understanding in order that I may know your commands; strengthen my heart against the snares of the enemy; enkindle my will. I have heard your voice, and I do not want

---

11. Cf. Col 1: 24: *pro corpore eius, quod est Ecclesia.*

to harden my heart and resist, saying, "Later… tomorrow." *Nunc cœpi!* Right now! Lest there be no tomorrow for me.

O Spirit of truth and of wisdom, Spirit of understanding and of counsel, Spirit of joy and of peace! I want what you want, because you want it, as you want it, when you want it.

Consideration

Our faith in the Holy Spirit: necessarily complete

"The arm of the Lord has not been shortened."[12] God is no less powerful today than he was in other times; his love for us is no less true. Our faith teaches us that all creation, the movement of the earth and the other heavenly bodies, the good actions of creatures and all the good that has been achieved in history—in short, everything—comes from God and is directed toward him.

The action of the Holy Spirit can pass unnoticed, because God does not reveal to us his plans, and because man's sin clouds over the divine gifts. But faith reminds us that God is always acting. He has created us and maintains us in existence, and he leads all creation by his grace toward the glorious freedom of the children of God.[13]

For this reason, Christian tradition has summarized the attitude that we should adopt toward the Holy Spirit in just one idea: docility. This means that we should be aware of the work of the Holy Spirit all around us and that in our own selves we should recognize the gifts he distributes, the movements and institutions he inspires, the affections and decisions he provokes in our hearts. The Holy Spirit carries out in the world the works of God. He is, as we read in a liturgical hymn, the giver of grace, the light of our hearts, the soul's guest, our rest in work, our consolation in sorrow. Without his help there is nothing innocent or valuable in man, because he is the one who cleanses the soiled, heals what is sick, sets on fire what is cold, straightens what is bent, and guides men toward the safe harbor of salvation and eternal joy.[14]

But our faith in the Holy Spirit must be complete—not just a vague belief in his presence in the world, but a grateful acceptance of the signs and realities into which he has poured forth his power in a spe-

---

12. Is 59: 1: *Non est abbreviata manus Domini.*
13. Cf. Rom 8: 21.
14. Cf. the Sequence *Veni Sancte Spiritus*, Mass of Pentecost Sunday.

cial way. When the Spirit of truth comes, our Lord tells us, "he will glorify me, for he will take of what is mine and declare it to you."[15] The Holy Spirit is the Spirit sent by Christ to carry out in us the work of holiness that our Lord merited for us on earth.

And so there cannot be faith in the Holy Spirit if there is not faith in Christ, in his sacraments, in his Church. One cannot act in accordance with one's Christian faith, cannot truly believe in the Holy Spirit, without loving the Church and trusting it. A man cannot be a coherent Christian if he limits himself to pointing out the deficiencies and limitations of some who represent the Church—if he judges her from the outside, as though he were not her son. Consider, moreover, the extraordinary importance and abundance of the Paraclete when the priest renews the sacrifice of Calvary by celebrating Mass on our altars.

Concluding Prayer

Holy and divine Spirit! Through the intercession of the Blessed Virgin Mary, your spouse, bring the fullness of your gifts into our hearts. Comforted and strengthened by you, may we live according to your will and may we die praising your infinite mercy. Through Christ our Lord. Amen.

FIFTH DAY

Introductory Prayer

Come, O Holy Spirit! Enlighten my understanding in order that I may know your commands; strengthen my heart against the snares of the enemy; enkindle my will. I have heard your voice, and I do not want to harden my heart and resist, saying, "Later… tomorrow." *Nunc cœpi!* Right now! Lest there be no tomorrow for me.

O Spirit of truth and of wisdom, Spirit of understanding and of counsel, Spirit of joy and of peace! I want what you want, because you want it, as you want it, when you want it.

---

15. John 16: 14.

Consideration

The Holy Spirit: present among us

We Christians carry the great treasures of grace in vessels of clay.[16] God has entrusted his gifts to the weakness and fragility of human freedom. We can be certain of the help of God's power, but our lust, our love of comfort, and our pride sometimes cause us to reject his grace and to fall into sin. For more than twenty-five years, when I have recited the Creed and asserted my faith in the divine origin of the Church as "one, holy, catholic, and apostolic," I have frequently added, "in spite of everything." When I mention this custom of mine and someone asks me what I mean, I answer, "I mean your sins and mine."

All this is true, but it does not authorize us in any way to judge the Church in a human manner, without theological faith. We cannot consider only the greater or lesser merits of certain churchmen or other Christians. To do this would be to limit ourselves to the surface of things. *What is most important in the Church is not how we humans react, but how God acts.* This is what the Church is: Christ present in our midst, God coming toward us in order to save us, calling us with his revelation, sanctifying us with his grace, maintaining us with his constant help, in the great and small battles of our daily life.

We might come to mistrust other people, and we should each mistrust ourselves (and end each day with a *mea culpa*, an act of contrition that is profound and sincere). But we have no right to doubt God. And to doubt the Church, its divine origin and its effectiveness for our salvation through its doctrine and its sacraments, would be the same as doubting God himself, the same as not fully believing in the reality of the coming of the Holy Spirit.

"Before Christ was crucified," writes St. John Chrysostom, "there was no reconciliation. And while there was no reconciliation, the Holy Spirit was not sent. . . . The absence of the Holy Spirit was a sign of the anger of God. Now that you see him sent in fullness, do not doubt the reconciliation. But what if people should ask, 'Where is the Holy Spirit now? We can talk of his presence when the miracles took place, when the dead were raised and the lepers were healed. But how are we to know that he is truly present now?' Do not be concerned. I will show you that the Holy Spirit is present among us now as well.

16. Cf. 2 Cor 4: 7.

"If the Holy Spirit were not present, we would not be able to say, 'Jesus is the Lord,' for no one can invoke Jesus as the Lord unless it is in the Holy Spirit (1 Cor 12: 3). If the Holy Spirit were not present, we would not be able to pray with confidence. For when we pray, we say, 'Our Father, who art in heaven' (Mt 6: 9). If the Holy Spirit were not present, we could not call God our Father. How do we know this? Because the apostle teaches us: 'And, because you are his children, God has sent the Spirit of his Son into our hearts, crying, "Abba! Father!"' (Gal 4: 6).

"When you call on God the Father, remember that it is the Spirit who, with his motion in your soul, has given you this prayer. If the Holy Spirit were not present, there would be no word of wisdom or knowledge in the Church; for it is written, 'The word of wisdom is given through the Spirit' (1 Cor 12: 8).... If the Holy Spirit were not present, the Church would not exist. But if the Church exists, there is no doubt of the presence of the Holy Spirit."[17]

Beyond all human deficiencies and limitations, the Church is the sign and, in a certain sense, though not in the strict sense in which the Church has defined the nature of the seven sacraments of the new law, the universal sacrament of the presence of God in the world. To be a Christian is to be reborn of God and sent to announce the news of salvation. If we had a strong faith, a living faith, if we were bold in making Christ known to others, we would see with our own eyes miracles such as those that took place in the time of the apostles.

Today, too, the blind who have lost the ability to look up to heaven and contemplate the wonderful works of God recover their sight. The lame and the crippled who have been bound by their passions, and whose hearts have forgotten love, recover their freedom. The deaf who did not want to know God are given back their hearing. The dumb whose tongues were bound because they did not want to acknowledge their defeats begin to talk. And the dead in whom sin had destroyed life come to life again. We see once more that "the word of God is living and active, sharper than any two-edged sword."[18] And, just as the first Christians did, we rejoice when we contemplate the power of the Holy

---

17. St. John Chrysostom, *Sermones panegyrici in solemnitates D. N. Iesu Christi*, homily I, *De Sancta Pentecoste* 3-4.

18. Heb 4: 12.

Spirit and see the results of his action on the minds and wills of his creatures.

Concluding Prayer

Holy and divine Spirit! Through the intercession of the Blessed Virgin Mary, your spouse, bring the fullness of your gifts into our hearts. Comforted and strengthened by you, may we live according to your will and may we die praising your infinite mercy. Through Christ our Lord. Amen.

SIXTH DAY

Introductory Prayer

Come, O Holy Spirit! Enlighten my understanding in order that I may know your commands; strengthen my heart against the snares of the enemy; enkindle my will. I have heard your voice, and I do not want to harden my heart and resist, saying, "Later... tomorrow." *Nunc cœpi!* Right now! Lest there be no tomorrow for me.

O Spirit of truth and of wisdom, Spirit of understanding and of counsel, Spirit of joy and of peace! I want what you want, because you want it, as you want it, when you want it.

Consideration

The action of the Holy Spirit: teaching how to correspond to it

I see all the circumstances of life—those of every individual person's existence, as well as, in some way, those of the great crossroads of history—as so many calls that God makes to men, to bring them face to face with truth, and as occasions that are offered to us Christians, so that we may announce, with our deeds and with our words strengthened by grace, the Spirit to whom we belong.[19]

Every generation of Christians needs to redeem, to sanctify its own time. In order to do this, we must understand and share the desires of other men—as equals—in order to make known to them, with a *gift of tongues*, how they are to correspond to the action of the Holy Spirit, to that permanent outflow of rich treasures that comes from our Lord's heart. We Christians are called upon to announce, in our own

---

19. Cf. Rom 8: 9-13.

time, to this world to which we belong and in which we live, the message—old and at the same time new—of the Gospel.

It is not true that everyone today, in general, is closed or indifferent to what our Christian faith teaches about man's being and destiny. It is not true that men in our time are turned toward only the things of this earth and have forgotten to look up to heaven. There is no lack of narrow ideologies, it is true, or of persons who maintain them. But in our time we find both great desires and base attitudes, heroism and cowardice, zeal and disenchantment: those who dream of a new world, more just and more human, and others who—discouraged, perhaps, by the failure of their youthful idealism—hide themselves in the selfishness of seeking only their own security or remaining immersed in their errors.

To all these men and women, wherever they may be, in their more exalted moments or in their crises and defeats, we have to bring the solemn and unequivocal message of St. Peter in the days that followed Pentecost: Jesus is the cornerstone, the Redeemer, the hope of our lives. "For there is no other name under heaven given to men by which we must be saved."[20]

Concluding Prayer

Holy and divine Spirit! Through the intercession of the Blessed Virgin Mary, your spouse, bring the fullness of your gifts into our hearts. Comforted and strengthened by you, may we live according to your will and may we die praising your infinite mercy. Through Christ our Lord. Amen.

SEVENTH DAY

Introductory Prayer

Come, O Holy Spirit! Enlighten my understanding in order that I may know your commands; strengthen my heart against the snares of the enemy; enkindle my will. I have heard your voice, and I do not want to harden my heart and resist, saying, "Later … tomorrow." *Nunc cœpi!* Right now! Lest there be no tomorrow for me.

---

20. Acts 4: 12.

O Spirit of truth and of wisdom, Spirit of understanding and of counsel, Spirit of joy and of peace! I want what you want, because you want it, as you want it, when you want it.

Consideration

The gift of wisdom: making us know
God and rejoice in his presence

I would say that, among the gifts of the Holy Spirit, there is one which we all need in a special way: the gift of wisdom. It makes us know God and rejoice in his presence, thereby placing us in a perspective from which we can judge accurately the situations and events of this life. If we were consistent with our faith when we looked around us and contemplated the world and its history, we would be unable to avoid feeling in our own hearts the same sentiments that filled the heart of our Lord: "Seeing the crowds, he was moved with compassion for them, because they were bewildered and dejected, like sheep without a shepherd."[21]

Not that the Christian should neglect to see all that is good in humanity, to appreciate its healthy joys, or to participate in its enthusiasm and ideals. On the contrary, a true Christian will vibrate in unison with all the good he finds in the world. And he will live in the midst of it with a special concern, because of knowing, better than anyone, the depth and the richness of the human spirit.

A Christian's faith does not diminish his spirit or limit the noble impulses of his soul—rather, it makes them grow with the realization of their true and authentic meaning. We do not exist in order to pursue just any happiness. We have been called to penetrate the intimacy of God's own life, to know and love God the Father, God the Son, and God the Holy Spirit, and to love also—in that same love of the one God in three divine Persons—the angels and all men.

This is the great boldness of the Christian faith: to proclaim the value and dignity of human nature and to affirm that we have been created to achieve the dignity of children of God, through the grace that raises us up to a supernatural level. An incredible boldness it would be, were it not founded on the promise of salvation given us by God the Father,

---

21. Mt 9: 36.

confirmed by the blood of Christ, and reaffirmed and made possible by the constant action of the Holy Spirit.

We must live by faith. We must grow in faith, up to the point where it will be possible to describe any one of us in the terms used by one of the great Doctors of the Eastern Church to describe Christians in general: "In the same way that a transparent body, upon receiving a ray of light, becomes resplendent and shines out, so the souls that are borne and illuminated by the Holy Spirit become themselves spiritual and carry to others the light of grace. From the Holy Spirit comes knowledge of future events, understanding of mysteries, comprehension of hidden truths, giving of gifts, heavenly citizenship, conversation with the angels. From him comes never-ending joy, perseverance in God, likeness to God, and the most sublime state that can be conceived, that of becoming God-like."[22]

Together with humility, the realization of the greatness of man's dignity—and of the overwhelming fact that, by grace, we are made children of God—forms a single attitude. It is not our own forces that save us and give us life; it is the grace of God. This is a truth which can never be forgotten. If it were, the *divinization* of our life would be perverted and would become presumption, pride. And this would lead, sooner or later, to a breakdown of spiritual life, when the soul came face to face with its own weakness and wretchedness.

"And shall I dare to say, 'I am holy'?" asks St. Augustine. "If I mean by 'holy' that I bring holiness and that I need no one to make me holy, I would be a liar and full of pride. But if by 'holy' I understand that one is made holy, as we read in Leviticus, 'You will be holy, because I, God, am holy,' then the whole body of Christ, down to the last person living at the ends of the earth, may dare to say, together with its head and under him, 'I am holy.'"[23]

Love the Third Person of the Most Blessed Trinity. Listen in the intimacy of your being to the divine motions of encouragement or reproach you receive from him. Walk through the world in the light that is poured out in your soul. And the God of hope will fill you with all peace, so that this hope may grow in you more and more each day, by the power of the Holy Spirit.[24]

---

22. St. Basil, *De Spiritu Sancto* 9, 23.

23. St. Augustine, *Enarrationes in psalmos* 85, 4.

Concluding Prayer

Holy and divine Spirit! Through the intercession of the Blessed Virgin Mary, your spouse, bring the fullness of your gifts into our hearts. Comforted and strengthened by you, may we live according to your will and may we die praising your infinite mercy. Through Christ our Lord. Amen.

EIGHTH DAY

Introductory Prayer

Come, O Holy Spirit! Enlighten my understanding in order that I may know your commands; strengthen my heart against the snares of the enemy; enkindle my will. I have heard your voice, and I do not want to harden my heart and resist, saying, "Later ... tomorrow." *Nunc cœpi!* Right now! Lest there be no tomorrow for me.

O Spirit of truth and of wisdom, Spirit of understanding and of counsel, Spirit of joy and of peace! I want what you want, because you want it, as you want it, when you want it.

Consideration

The Holy Spirit: living according to him

To live according to the Holy Spirit means to live by faith and hope and charity — to allow God to take possession of our lives and to change our hearts, to make us resemble him more and more. A mature and profound Christian life cannot be improvised, because it is the result of the growth of God's grace in us. In the Acts of the Apostles we find the early Christian community described in a single sentence that is brief but full of meaning: "And they continued steadfastly in the teaching of the apostles and in the communion of the breaking of the bread and in prayers."[25]

This is how the early Christians lived, and this is how we, too, should live: meditating upon the doctrine of our faith until it becomes a part of us; receiving our Lord in the Eucharist; meeting him in the personal dialogue of our prayer, not trying to hide behind an impersonal kind of conduct, but coming face to face with him. These means should be-

---

24. Cf. Rom 15: 13.
25. Acts 2: 42.

come the very substance of our attitude. If they are lacking, we shall have, perhaps, the ability to think in an erudite manner, an activity that is more or less intense, some practices and devotions. But we shall not have an authentically Christian way of life, because we will lack that personal relationship with Christ, which is a real and living participation in the divine work of salvation. This is a teaching that applies to any Christian, because we are all, equally, called to sanctity. There are no second-class Christians, obliged to practice only a "simplified version" of the Gospel. We have all received the same Baptism, and although there is a great variety of spiritual gifts and human situations, there is only one Spirit who distributes God's gifts, only one faith, only one hope, only one love.[26]

And so we can apply to ourselves the question asked by the apostle: "Do you not know that you are the temple of God, and that the Spirit of God dwells in you?"[27] And we can understand it as an invitation to deal with God in a more personal and direct manner. For some, unfortunately, the Paraclete is the Great Stranger, the Great Unknown. He is merely a name that is mentioned, but not Someone, not one of the three Persons (in the one God) with whom we can talk and with whose life we can live.

We have to deal with him simply and trustingly, as we are taught by the Church in its liturgy. Then we will come to know our Lord better, and at the same time we will realize more fully the great favor that has been granted us when we became Christians. We will see all the greatness and truth of the *divinization* to which I referred earlier, which is a sharing in God's own life.

Concluding Prayer

Holy and divine Spirit! Through the intercession of the Blessed Virgin Mary, your spouse, bring the fullness of your gifts into our hearts. Comforted and strengthened by you, may we live according to your will and may we die praising your infinite mercy. Through Christ our Lord. Amen.

---

26. Cf. 1 Cor 12: 4-6; 13: 1-13.
27. 1 Cor 3: 16.

NINTH DAY

Introductory Prayer

Come, O Holy Spirit! Enlighten my understanding in order that I may know your commands; strengthen my heart against the snares of the enemy; enkindle my will. I have heard your voice, and I do not want to harden my heart and resist, saying, "Later... tomorrow." *Nunc cœpi!* Right now! Lest there be no tomorrow for me.

O Spirit of truth and of wisdom, Spirit of understanding and of counsel, Spirit of joy and of peace! I want what you want, because you want it, as you want it, when you want it.

Consideration

Docility, a life of prayer, and union with the cross:
fundamental points

"The Holy Spirit is not an artist who draws the divine substance in us, as though he were alien to it. It is not in this way that he leads us to a resemblance with God—but rather, being God and proceeding from God, he himself marks the hearts of those who receive him, as a seal upon wax. In this way, by the communication of his own life and resemblance, he restores nature according to the beauty of the divine model, and returns to us our resemblance to God."[28]

Let us see how this truth applies to our daily lives. Let us describe, at least in general, the way of life which will bring us to deal in a familiar manner with the Holy Spirit, and, together with him, the Father and the Son.

We can fix our attention on three fundamental points: docility, a life of prayer, and union with the cross.

First of all, docility, because it is the Holy Spirit who, with his inspirations, gives a supernatural tone to our thoughts, desires, and actions. It is he who leads us to receive Christ's teaching and to assimilate it in a profound way. It is he who gives us the light by which we perceive our personal calling and the strength to carry out all that God expects of us. If we are docile to the Holy Spirit, the image of Christ will be formed more and more fully in us, and we will be brought closer every

---

28. St. Cyril of Alexandria, *Thesaurus de sancta et consubstantiali Trinitate* 34.

day to God the Father. "For whoever are led by the Spirit of God, they are the children of God."[29]

If we let ourselves be guided by this life-giving principle, the Holy Spirit in us, our spiritual vitality will grow. We will place ourselves in the hands of our Father God, with the same spontaneity and confidence with which children abandon themselves to their fathers' care. Our Lord has said: "Unless you become like little children, you will not enter the kingdom of heaven."[30] This is the old and well-known "way of childhood," which is not sentimentality or lack of human maturity. It is a supernatural maturity, which makes us realize more deeply the wonders of God's love, while leading us to acknowledge our own smallness and identify our will fully with the will of God.

In the second place, a life of prayer, because the giving of one's self, the obedience and meekness of a Christian, are born of love and lead to love. And love leads to a personal relationship, to conversation and friendship. Christian life requires a constant dialogue with God—one in three Persons—and it is to this intimacy that the Holy Spirit leads us. "For who among men knows the things of a man save the spirit of the man which is in him? Even so, the things of God no one knows but the Spirit of God."[31] If we have a constant relationship with the Holy Spirit, we ourselves will become spiritual, we will realize that we are Christ's brothers and children of God, and we will not hesitate to call upon our Father at any time.[32]

Let us acquire the habit of conversation with the Holy Spirit, who is the one who will make us holy. Let us trust in him and ask his help and feel his closeness to us. In this way our poor hearts will grow; we will have a greater desire to love God and to love all creatures for God's sake. And our lives will reproduce that final vision of the Apocalypse: the Spirit and the Spouse, the Holy Spirit and the Church—and every Christian—calling on Jesus Christ to come and be with us for ever.[33]

---

29. Rom 8: 14.

30. Mt 18: 3.

31. 1 Cor 2: 11.

32. Cf. Rom 8: 15; Gal 4: 6.

33. Cf. Rev 22: 17.

And, finally, union with the cross, because in the life of Christ the Resurrection and Pentecost were preceded by Calvary. This is the order that must be followed in the life of any Christian. We are, as St. Paul tells us, "heirs indeed of God and joint heirs with Christ, provided, however, we suffer with him, that we may also be glorified with him."[34] The Holy Spirit comes to us as a result of the cross — as a result of our total abandonment to the will of God, of our seeking only his glory and renouncing ourselves completely.

Only when we are faithful to grace and determined to place the cross in the center of our soul, denying ourselves for the love of God, detaching ourselves in a real way from all selfishness and false human security, only then — when we live by faith in a real way — will we receive the fullness of the great fire, the great light, the great comfort of the Holy Spirit.

It is then, too, that the soul begins to experience the peace and freedom which Christ has won for us,[35] and which are given to us with the grace of the Holy Spirit. "The fruit of the Spirit is: charity, joy, peace, patience, kindness, goodness, long-suffering, mildness, faith, modesty, continency, chastity"[36] and "where the Spirit of the Lord is, there is freedom."[37]

Concluding Prayer

Holy and divine Spirit! Through the intercession of the Blessed Virgin Mary, your spouse, bring the fullness of your gifts into our hearts. Comforted and strengthened by you, may we live according to your will and may we die praising your infinite mercy. Through Christ our Lord. Amen.

---

34. Rom 8: 17.
35. Cf. Gal 4: 31.
36. Cf. Gal 5: 22-23.
37. 2 Cor 3: 17.

TENTH DAY

Introductory Prayer

Come, O Holy Spirit! Enlighten my understanding in order that I may know your commands; strengthen my heart against the snares of the enemy; enkindle my will. I have heard your voice, and I do not want to harden my heart and resist, saying, "Later... tomorrow." *Nunc cœpi!* Right now! Lest there be no tomorrow for me.

O Spirit of truth and of wisdom, Spirit of understanding and of counsel, Spirit of joy and of peace! I want what you want, because you want it, as you want it, when you want it.

Consideration

Beginning and beginning again

In the midst of the limitations that accompany our present life, in which sin is still present in us to some extent at least, we Christians perceive with a particular clearness all the wealth of our divine filiation, when we realize that we are fully free because we are doing our Father's work, when our joy becomes constant because no one can take our hope away. It is then that we can admire at the same time all the great and beautiful things of this earth, can appreciate the richness and goodness of creation, and can love with all the strength and purity for which the human heart was made. It is then that sorrow for sin does not degenerate into a bitter gesture of despair or pride, because sorrow and knowledge of human weakness lead us to identify ourselves again with Christ's work of redemption and feel more deeply our solidarity with others.

It is then, finally, that we Christians experience in our own life the sure strength of the Holy Spirit, in such a way that our own failures do not drag us down. Rather, they are an invitation to begin again and to continue being faithful witnesses of Christ in all the moments of our life—in spite of our own personal weaknesses, which, in such a case, are normally no more than small failings that hardly perturb the soul. And even if they are grave sins, the sacrament of Penance, received with true sorrow, enables us to recover our peace with God and to become again a good witness of his mercy.

Such is the brief summary, which can barely be expressed in human language, of the richness of our faith and of our Christian life, if we let ourselves be guided by the Holy Spirit. That is why I can end these words in only one way: by voicing a prayer, contained in one of the liturgical hymns for the feast of Pentecost, which is like an echo of the unceasing petition of the whole Church: "Come, creating Spirit, to the minds of those who belong to you, and fill, with grace from above, the hearts that you have created.... Grant that through you we may know the Father and become acquainted with the Son; may we believe in you, the Spirit who proceeds from the Father and Son, for ever. Amen."[38]

Concluding Prayer

Holy and divine Spirit! Through the intercession of the Blessed Virgin Mary, your spouse, bring the fullness of your gifts into our hearts. Comforted and strengthened by you, may we live according to your will and may we die praising your infinite mercy. Through Christ our Lord. Amen.

---

38. Hymn *Veni, Creator*, Divine Office of Pentecost Sunday.

VENI CREATOR
(COME, HOLY SPIRIT, CREATOR)

Veni, Creátor Spíritus,
mentes tuórum vísita,
imple supérna grátia,
quæ tu creásti, péctora.

Qui díceris Paráclitus,
donum Dei altíssimi,
fons vivus, ignis, cáritas
et spiritális únctio.

Tu septifórmis múnere,
dextræ Dei tu dígitus,
tu rite promíssum Patris
sermóne ditans gúttura.

Accénde lumen sénsibus,
infúnde amórem córdibus,
infírma nostri córporis
virtúte firmans pérpeti.

Hostem repéllas lóngius
pacémque dones prótinus;
ductóre sic te prævio
vitémus omne nóxium.

Per te sciámus da Patrem
noscámus atque Fílium,
te utriúsque Spíritum
credámus omni témpore.

Deo Patris sit glória,
Et Fílio, qui a mórtuis
surréxit, ac Paráclito
in sæculórum sæcula.
Amen.

Come, Holy Spirit, Creator, come
From thy bright heavenly throne!
Come, take possession of our souls,
And make them all thine own!

Thou who art called the Paraclete,
Best gift of God above,
The living spring, the living fire,
Sweet unction, and true love!

Thou who art sevenfold in thy grace,
Finger of God's right hand,
His promise, teaching little ones
To speak and understand!

O guide our minds with thy blest light,
With love our hearts inflame,
And with thy strength which ne'er decays
Confirm our mortal frame.

Far from us drive our hellish foe,
True peace unto us bring,
And through all perils guide us safe
Beneath thy sacred wing.

Through thee may we the Father know,
Through thee, the eternal Son,
And thee, the Spirit of them both,
Thrice-blessed Three in one.

All glory to the Father be,
And to the risen Son;
The same to thee, O Paraclete,
While endless ages run.
Amen.

℣. Emítte Spíritum tuum
et creabúntur.

℟. **Et renovábis
fáciem terræ.**

Orémus.

Deus, qui corda fidélium
Sancti Spíritus illustratióne
docuísti; da nobis in eódem
Spíritu recta sápere; et de eius
semper consolatióne gaudére.
Per Christum Dóminum
nostrum.

℟. **Amen.**

℣. Send forth thy Spirit,
and they shall be created.

℟. **And thou shalt renew
the face of the earth.**

Let us pray.

O God, who hast taught the hearts
of the faithful by the light of the
Holy Spirit, grant that by the gift
of the same Spirit we may be
always truly wise and ever rejoice
in his consolation. Through Christ
our Lord.

℟. **Amen.**

PRAYER IN THE OCTAVE OF CHRISTIAN UNITY

This prayer is said each day from January 18 to 25.

May they all be one, as you, Father, are in me, and I in you; so that
the world may come to believe that it is you who has sent me.

℣. You are Peter.

℟. **And it is upon this rock that I will build my Church.**

Let us pray.

Lord Jesus Christ, who said to your apostles: I leave peace with you;
it is my own peace that I give you; look not upon our sins but upon
your Church's faith, and graciously grant her peace and unity in
accordance with your will. You who live and reign for ever and ever.

℟. **Amen.**

DEVOTIONS TO
THE BLESSED VIRGIN MARY

"'All generations will call me blessed': 'The Church's devotion to the Blessed Virgin is intrinsic to Christian worship.' The Church rightly honors 'the Blessed Virgin with special devotion. From the most ancient times the Blessed Virgin has been honored with the title of "Mother of God," to whose protection the faithful fly in all their dangers and needs.... This very special devotion . . . differs essentially from the adoration which is given to the incarnate Word and equally to the Father and the Holy Spirit, and greatly fosters this adoration.' The liturgical feasts dedicated to the Mother of God and Marian prayer, such as the Rosary, an 'epitome of the whole Gospel,' express this devotion to the Virgin Mary."[1]

THE HOLY ROSARY

The Rosary is a centuries-old way of praying. "Medieval piety in the West developed the prayer of the Rosary as a popular substitute for the Liturgy of the Hours." Although obviously Marian in character, it is Christ-centered in its essentials. It is a meditation on the lives of both our Lord and the Virgin Mary. "Christian prayer tries above all to meditate on the mysteries of Christ, as in . . . the Rosary."

"Meditation engages thought, imagination, emotion, and desire. This mobilization of faculties is necessary in order to deepen our convictions of faith, prompt the conversion of our heart, and strengthen our will to follow Christ."

Meditation upon these mysteries leads us to contemplation: "This form of prayerful reflection is of great value, but Christian prayer should go further: to the knowledge of the love of the Lord Jesus, to union with him."[2]

The Rosary has a structure and method designed to help us more readily assimilate the mysteries into our spiritual life. Structurally, it is divided into four parts; each part, into five mysteries. For each

---

1. CCC 971; Lk 1: 48; MC 42, 56; LG 66; SC 103.
2. CCC 2678, 2708.

mystery is said one "decade" consisting of one Our Father, ten Hail Marys and one Glory be.

Though at first sight this method of repetition may seem to be tedious and boring, it is better understood when considered as an act of love: "when the Rosary is thought of as an outpouring of that love which tirelessly returns to the person loved with expressions similar in their content but ever fresh in terms of the feeling pervading them."[3]

It is also important to remember that though these repeated invocations are directed to Mary, our acts of love are ultimately directed to Jesus himself, through her intercession. In many Catholic families, there is a pious custom of reciting daily one part of the Rosary.

Structure of the Rosary

Make the Sign of the Cross:

In the name of the Father, and of the Son, and of the Holy Spirit. Amen.

There are, at present, many legitimate ways of introducing the Rosary, in different parts of the Church and following different customs. They should all appropriately prepare the mind for contemplation. The beginning of Psalm 70 is frequently used: "O God, come to my aid; O Lord, make haste to help me." Also common is the recitation of the Apostles' Creed:

I believe in God,
the Father almighty,
Creator of heaven and earth,
and in Jesus Christ, his only Son, our Lord,
who was conceived by the Holy Spirit,
born of the Virgin Mary,
suffered under Pontius Pilate,
was crucified, died and was buried;
he descended into hell;
on the third day he rose again from the dead;
he ascended into heaven,
and is seated at the right hand of God the Father almighty;
from there he will come to judge the living and the dead.

---

3. RVM 26.

I believe in the Holy Spirit,
the holy catholic Church,
the communion of saints,
the forgiveness of sins,
the resurrection of the body,
and life everlasting. Amen.

Then, for an increase in the virtues of faith, hope, and charity:

Our Father. Three Hail Marys. Glory be.

Now, begin the mysteries of the day. Start each decade by announcing the mystery and directing your imagination and attention towards that particular episode in the life of Christ or our Lady.

It can be useful to follow the announcement of the mystery with the reading of a related scriptural passage, as indicated below. In this way, the Rosary is not merely a matter of recalling information but of allowing God to speak to you directly through his word.

Ideally, this should be followed by a period of silence, in which to reflect upon the scripture passage before moving on to vocal prayer.

Then proceed to the recitation of the decade. On the large bead say the **Our Father**. On each of the ten small beads, say a **Hail Mary**. Then pray the **Glory be**.

Each decade is a contemplation of the life of our Lord, witnessed by Mary—one aspect of the paschal mystery. In recognition of the connection with Christian life, one should conclude one's contemplation of each of them with a prayer for the fruits specific to that particular mystery. Alternatively, a more general prayer may be said, according to custom, such as the following:

O my Jesus, forgive us our sins, save us from the fire of hell, draw all souls to heaven, especially those who are in most need of your mercy.

or:

Mary, mother of grace, mother of mercy, shield me from the enemy and receive me at the hour of my death. Amen.

At the end of the Rosary any suitable prayers may be said, though the following are the most common: the **Hail Holy Queen** (pp.170–171) followed by the prayer O God, whose only-begotten Son... (p.155); or *Sub Tuum Præsidium* (We Fly to Your Patronage) (p.153) followed by the Litany of the Blessed Virgin Mary (p.153).

Mysteries of the Rosary

Joyful   MONDAYS AND SATURDAYS
1. The Annunciation (Lk 1: 26-38)
2. The Visitation (Lk 1: 39-56)
3. The Nativity (Lk 2: 1-20)
4. The Presentation (Lk 2: 22-38)
5. The Finding of Jesus in the Temple (Lk 2: 41-52)

Luminous   THURSDAYS
1. The Baptism of Christ in the Jordan (Mt 3: 13-17; Mk 1: 4-11)
2. The Manifestation of Christ at the wedding of Cana (Jn 2: 1-11)
3. The Proclamation of the Kingdom of God, and his call to
   conversion (Mt 4: 12-25; Mk 1: 15; 2: 3-13; Lk 7: 47-48;
   Jn 20: 22-23)
4. The Transfiguration (Mt 17: 1-9 / Lk 9: 28-36)
5. The Institution of the Eucharist (Lk 22: 14-20; Jn 13: 1)

Sorrowful   TUESDAYS AND FRIDAYS
1. The Agony in the Garden (Mt 26: 36-56)
2. The Scourging at the Pillar (Is 53: 1-12; Mk 15: 1-15)
3. The Crowning with Thorns (Mk 15: 16-20; Mt 27: 27-31)
4. The Carrying of the Cross (Lk 23: 26-32; Mk 10: 17-21)
5. The Crucifixion (Jn 19: 17-30; Mt 27: 35-56)

Glorious   WEDNESDAYS AND SUNDAYS
1. The Resurrection (Mt 28: 1-15; Lk 24: 1-49; Mk 16: 1-18)
2. The Ascension (Acts 1: 3-11)
3. The Descent of the Holy Spirit (Acts 2: 1-21)
4. The Assumption (Rev 12: 1)
5. The Coronation of the Blessed Virgin Mary (Lk 1: 46-55)

SUB TUUM PRÆSIDIUM
(WE FLY TO YOUR PATRONAGE)

We fly to your patronage, O holy Mother of God. Despise not our petitions in our necessities, but deliver us from all dangers, O ever-glorious and blessed Virgin.

LITANY OF THE BLESSED VIRGIN MARY

The litany is a way of praying found among many peoples. It is a prayer made to be repeated; one phrase coming over and over again, so that the person praying is caught up in the prayer itself. Often litanies are chanted.

The Litany of the Blessed Virgin Mary (called the Litany of Loreto, also) took shape over several centuries. It is rooted in images that we find in the Scriptures. It may be said after praying the Rosary.

Lord, have mercy on us.	**Christ, have mercy on us.**
Lord, have mercy on us, Christ, hear us.	**Christ graciously hear us.**

God the Father of heaven,	**Have mercy on us.**
God the Son, Redeemer of the world,	**Have mercy on us.**
God the Holy Spirit,	**Have mercy on us.**
Holy Trinity, one God,	**Have mercy on us.**

Holy Mary,	**Pray for us.**

Holy Mother of God…
Holy Virgin of virgins…
Mother of Christ…
Mother of the Church…
Mother of divine grace…
Mother most pure…
Mother most chaste…
Mother inviolate…
Mother undefiled…
Mother most amiable…
Mother most admirable…
Mother of good counsel…
Mother of our Creator…

Mother of our Savior, **pray for us.**
Virgin most prudent...
Virgin most venerable...
Virgin most renowned...
Virgin most powerful...
Virgin most merciful...
Virgin most faithful...
Mirror of justice...
Seat of wisdom...
Cause of our joy...
Spiritual vessel...
Vessel of honor...
Singular vessel of devotion...
Mystical rose...
Tower of David...
Tower of ivory...
House of gold...
Ark of the Covenant...
Gate of Heaven...
Morning star...
Health of the sick...
Refuge of sinners...
Comforter of the afflicted...
Help of Christians...
Queen of angels...
Queen of patriarchs...
Queen of prophets...
Queen of apostles...
Queen of martyrs...
Queen of confessors...
Queen of virgins...
Queen of all saints...
Queen conceived without Original Sin...
Queen assumed into Heaven...
Queen of the most holy Rosary...
Queen of families...
Queen of peace...

℣. Lamb of God, you take away the sins of the world,

℟. **Spare us, O Lord.**

℣. Lamb of God, you take away the sins of the world,

℟. **Graciously hear us, O Lord.**

℣. Lamb of God, you take away the sins of the world,

℟. **Have mercy on us.**

℣. Pray for us, O holy Mother of God,

℟. **That we may be made worthy of the promises of Christ.**

Let us pray.

O God, whose only-begotten Son, by his life, death, and resurrection, has purchased for us the rewards of everlasting life; grant, we beseech you, that, we, who meditate on these mysteries of the most holy Rosary of the Blessed Virgin Mary, may imitate what they contain, and obtain what they promise. Through Christ our Lord.

℟. **Amen.**

There is also a custom of ending the Rosary with prayers for the intentions of the holy Father, the whole Church, the (arch)bishop of the diocese, and the holy souls in purgatory. The following prayers are suggested:

For the intentions of the Pope and the needs of the Church and of the nation:

Our Father. Hail Mary. Glory Be.

For the (arch)bishop of this (arch)diocese and his intentions:

Our Father. Hail Mary. Glory Be.

For the holy souls in Purgatory:

Our Father. Hail Mary. May they rest in peace.

℟. **Amen.**

Omnes ad Iesum per Mariam

MEDITATIONS ON THE
MYSTERIES OF THE ROSARY

The Rosary is one of the traditional paths of Christian prayer directed to the contemplation of Christ's face....

After the announcement of the mystery and the proclamation of the word, it is fitting to pause and focus one's attention for a suitable period of time on the mystery concerned, before moving into vocal prayer. A discovery of the importance of silence is one of the secrets of practicing contemplation and meditation. One drawback of a society dominated by technology and the mass media is the fact that silence becomes increasingly difficult to achieve. Just as moments of silence are recommended in the Liturgy, so too in the recitation of the Rosary it is fitting to pause briefly after listening to the word of God, while the mind focuses on the content of a particular mystery.[4]

The meditations that follow are from *Holy Rosary* (HR), written in 1931 by St. Josemaria Escriva. A meditation on the Luminous Mysteries did not appear in *Holy Rosary*, but throughout his life St. Josemaria lovingly contemplated and preached on these scenes, just as he did with every chapter of the Gospels. Therefore, we have included here some excerpts from among his writings that make reference to the Luminous Mysteries to help readers meditate on the complete Rosary.

JOYFUL MYSTERIES

1. THE ANNUNCIATION

Don't forget, my friend, that we are children. The Lady of the sweet name, Mary, is absorbed in prayer.

You, in that house, can be whatever you wish: a friend, a servant, an onlooker, a neighbor.... For the moment I don't dare to be anything. I hide behind you, and, full of awe, I watch what's happening.

The Archangel delivers his message.... *Quomodo fiet istud, quoniam virum non cognosco?*

---

4. St. John Paul II, Apostolic Letter *Rosarium Virginis Mariæ*, October 16, 2002. nos. 18, 31.

"But how can this come about, since I am a virgin?" (Lk 1: 34). Our mother's voice reminds me—by contrast—of all the impurities of men… mine too.

And then how I hate those low, mean things of the earth…. What resolutions!

Fiat mihi secundum verbum tuum. "Let it be done to me according to your word" (Lk 1: 38). At the enchantment of this virginal phrase, the Word became flesh.

The first decade is about to end…. I still have time to tell God, before anyone else does, "Jesus, I love you."

2. THE VISITATION

By now, my little friend, you have no doubt learned to manage on your own. Joyfully keep Joseph and Mary company… and you will hear the traditions of the House of David.

You will hear about Elizabeth and Zechariah, you will be moved by Joseph's pure love, and your heart will pound whenever they mention the Child who will be born in Bethlehem.

We walk in haste towards the mountains to a town of the tribe of Judah (Lk 1: 39).

We arrive. It is the house where John the Baptist is to be born. Elizabeth gratefully hails the mother of her Redeemer: "Blessed are you among women, and blessed is the fruit of your womb. Why should I be honored with a visit from the mother of my Lord?" (Lk 1: 42–43).

The unborn Baptist quivers… (Lk 1: 41). Mary's humility pours forth in the *Magnificat*…. And you and I, who are proud—who were proud—promise to be humble.

3. THE NATIVITY

Caesar Augustus has issued a decree for a census to be taken of the whole world. For this purpose, everyone must go to the city of his ancestors. And, since Joseph belongs to the house and line of David, he goes with the Virgin Mary from Nazareth to the town of David, called Bethlehem, in Judea (Lk 2: 1-5).

And in Bethlehem is born our God: Jesus Christ! There is no room in the inn; he is born in a stable. And his mother wraps him in swaddling clothes and lays him in a manger (Lk 2: 7).

Cold. Poverty.... I am Joseph's little servant. How good Joseph is! He treats me like a son. He even forgives me if I take the Child in my arms and spend hour after hour saying sweet and loving things to him.

And I kiss him—you kiss him, too!—and I rock him in my arms, and I sing to him and call him King, Love, my God, my Only-one, my All...! How beautiful is the Child ... and how short the decade!

4. THE PRESENTATION

When the time has come for the mother's purification, in accordance with the Law of Moses, the Child must be taken to Jerusalem to be presented to the Lord (Lk 2: 22).

And this time it will be you, my friend, who carries the cage with the doves (Lk 2: 24).

Just think: She—Mary Immaculate!—submits to the Law as if she were defiled.

Through this example, foolish child, won't you learn to fulfill the holy law of God regardless of any personal sacrifice?

Purification! You and I certainly do need purification.

Atonement and, more than atonement, love. Love as a searing iron to cauterize our soul's uncleanness, and as a fire to kindle with divine flames the wretchedness of our hearts.

An upright and devout man has come to the Temple, led by the Holy Spirit (it has been revealed to him that he would not die until he had set eyes on the Christ). He takes the Messiah into his arms and says: "Now, my Lord, you can let your servant go from this world in peace, just as you promised, because my eyes have seen the Savior" (Lk 2: 25-30).

5. THE FINDING OF THE CHILD JESUS IN THE TEMPLE

Where is Jesus? The Child, my Lady! Where is he?

Mary is crying. In vain you and I have run from group to group, from

caravan to caravan: no one has seen him. Joseph, after fruitless attempts to keep from crying, cries too.... And you.... And I.

Being a rough little fellow, I cry my eyes out and wail to heaven and earth... to make up for the times when I lost him through my own fault and did not cry.

Jesus: may I never lose you again.... Then you and I are united in misfortune and grief, as we were united in sin. And, from the depths of our being come sighs of heartfelt sorrow and burning phrases, which the pen cannot and should not record.

And, as we are consoled by the joy of finding Jesus—three days he was gone!—debating with the teachers of Israel (Lk 2: 46), you and I will be left deeply impressed by the duty to leave our home and family to serve our heavenly Father.

LUMINOUS MYSTERIES

1. BAPTISM OF OUR LORD

Then Jesus came from Galilee to the Jordan to John, to be baptized by him... and lo, a voice from heaven, saying, "This is my beloved Son, with whom I am well pleased" (Mt 3: 13, 17).

In Baptism, our Father God has taken possession of our lives. He has made us sharers in Christ's life and sent us the Holy Spirit.

The strength and the power of God light up the face of the earth.

We will set the world ablaze, with the flames of the fire that you came to enkindle on earth! And the light of your truth, our Jesus, will enlighten men's minds in an endless day.

I can hear you crying out, my King, in your strong and ardent voice: *ignem veni mittere in terram, et quid volo nisi ut accendatur?* I have come to bring fire to the earth, and would that it were already enkindled! And I answer, with my entire being, with all my senses and faculties: *ecce ego: quia vocasti me!* Here I am, because you have called me!

God has placed an indelible mark on your soul through Baptism: you are a child of God.

Child, are you not aflame with the desire to bring all men to love Him?

2. WEDDING FEAST AT CANA

Our Lady was a guest at one of those noisy country weddings attended by people from many different villages. Mary was the only one who noticed the wine was running out. Don't these scenes from Christ's life seem familiar to us? The greatness of God lives at the level of ordinary things. It is natural for a woman, a homemaker, to notice an oversight, to look after the little things that make life pleasant. And that is how Mary acted.

Do whatever he tells you.

Implete hydrias (Jn 2: 7), fill the jars. And the miracle takes place. Everything is so simple and ordinary. The servants carry out their job. The water is easy to find. And this is the first manifestation of our Lord's divinity. What is commonplace becomes something extraordinary, something supernatural, when we have the good will to heed what God is asking of us.

Lord, I want to abandon all my concerns into your generous hands. Our Mother—your Mother—will have let you hear those words, now as in Cana: "They have no wine! … "

If our faith is weak, we should turn to Mary. Because of the miracle at the marriage feast at Cana, which Christ performed at his Mother's request, *his disciples learned to believe in him* (Jn 2: 11). Our Mother is always interceding with her Son so that he may attend to our needs and show himself to us, so that we can cry out, "You are the Son of God."

Grant me, dear Jesus, the faith I truly desire. My Mother, sweet Lady, Mary most holy, make me really believe!

3. PROCLAMATION OF THE KINGDOM OF GOD

The kingdom of God is at hand; repent, and believe in the gospel (Mk 1: 15). *And all the crowd gathered about him, and he taught them* (Mk 2: 13).

Jesus sees the boats on the shore and gets into one of them. How naturally Jesus steps into the boat of each and everyone of us!

When you seek to draw close to our Lord, remember that he is always

very close to you, that he is in you: *regnum Dei intra vos est* (Lk 17: 21). The kingdom of God is within you. You will find him in your heart.

Christ should reign first and foremost in our soul. But in order for him to reign in me, I need his abundant grace. Only in that way can my every heartbeat and breath, my least intense look, my most ordinary word, my most basic feeling be transformed into a hosanna to Christ my king.

Duc in altum. Put out into deep water! Throw aside the pessimism that makes a coward of you. *Et laxate retia vestra in capturam.* And pay out your nets for a catch!

We have to place our trust in our Lord's words: get into the boat, take the oars, hoist the sails and launch out into this sea of the world which Christ gives us as an inheritance.

Et regni ejus non erit finis. His kingdom will have no end.

Doesn't it fill you with joy to work for such a kingdom?

4. TRANSFIGURATION OF OUR LORD

And he was transfigured before them, and his face shone like the sun, and his garments became white as light (Mt 17: 2).

Jesus, we want to see you, to speak to you! We want to contemplate you, immersed in the immensity of your beauty, in a contemplation that will never cease! It must be wonderful to see you, Jesus! It must be wonderful to see you and be wounded by your love!

And a voice from the cloud said, "This is my beloved Son, with whom I am well pleased; listen to him" (Mt 17: 5).

Lord, we are ready to heed whatever you want to tell us. Speak to us: we are attentive to your voice. May your words enkindle our will so that we launch out fervently to obey you.

Vultum tuum, Domine, requiram (Ps 26: 8). Lord, I long to see your face. I like to close my eyes and think that, when God wills, the moment will come when I will be able to see him, not as *in a mirror dimly, but...face to face* (1 Cor 13: 12). Yes, *my heart yearns for God, the living God. When shall I go and behold the face of God?* (Ps 41: 3).

5. INSTITUTION OF THE EUCHARIST

Now before the feast of the Passover, when Jesus knew that his hour had come to depart out of this world to the Father, having loved his own who were in the world, he loved them to the end (Jn 13: 1).

When our Lord instituted the Eucharist during the Last Supper, night had already fallen. The world had fallen into darkness, for the old rites, the old signs of God's infinite mercy to mankind, were going to be brought to fulfillment. The way was opening to a new dawn — the new Passover. The Eucharist was instituted during that night, preparing in advance for the morning of the resurrection.

Jesus has remained in the Eucharist for love ... for you.

He has remained, knowing how men would treat him ... and how you would treat him.

He has remained so that you could eat him, and visit him and tell him your concerns; and so that, by your prayer beside the tabernacle and by receiving him sacramentally, you could fall more in love each day, and help other souls, many souls, to follow the same path.

Good child: see how lovers on earth kiss the flowers, the letters, the mementos of those they love ...

Then you, how could you ever forget that you have him always at your side — yes, *Him*? How could you forget ... that you can eat him?

Lord, may I never again flutter along close to the ground. Illumined by the rays of the divine Sun — Christ — in the Eucharist, may my flight never be interrupted until I find repose in your Heart.

SORROWFUL MYSTERIES

1. THE AGONY IN THE GARDEN

"Pray that you may not enter into temptation." And Peter fell asleep.

And the other apostles. And you, little friend, fell asleep ... and I too was another sleepy-headed Peter.

Jesus, alone and sad, suffers and soaks the earth with his blood.

Kneeling on the hard ground, he perseveres in prayer. . . . He weeps for you . . . and for me. The weight of the sins of men overwhelms him.

Pater, si vis, transfer calicem istum a me: "Father, if you are willing, remove this cup from me.... Yet not my will, but yours be done" (Lk 22: 42).

An angel from heaven comforts him. Jesus is in agony. He continues *prolixius*, praying more intensely…. He comes over to us and finds us asleep: "Rise," he says again, "and pray that you may not enter into temptation" (Lk 22: 46).

Judas the traitor: a kiss. Peter's sword gleams in the night. Jesus speaks: "Have you come out as against a robber, with swords and clubs to capture me?" (Mk 14: 48).

We are cowards: we follow him from afar — but awake and praying. Prayer…. Prayer…

2. THE SCOURGING AT THE PILLAR

Pilate speaks: "It is your custom that I release one prisoner to you at the Passover. Whom shall I set free: Barabbas — a thief jailed with others for murder — or Jesus?" (Mt 27: 17). The crowd, spurred on by their rulers, cry: "Put this man to death and release Barabbas' (Lk 23: 18).

Pilate speaks again: "What shall I do, then, with Jesus who is called Christ?" (Mt 27: 22). *Crucifige eum:* "Crucify him!" (Mk 15: 14).

Pilate, for the third time, says to them: "Why, what evil has he done? I have found in him no crime deserving death" (Lk 23: 22).

The clamor of the mob grows louder: "Crucify him; Crucify him!" (Mk 15: 14).

And Pilate, wanting to please the crowd, releases Barabbas to them and orders Jesus to be scourged.

Bound to the pillar. Covered with wounds.

The blows of the lash sound upon his torn flesh, upon his undefiled flesh, which suffers for your sinful flesh. More blows. More fury. Still more…. It is a last extreme of human cruelty.

Finally, exhausted, they untie Jesus. And the body of Christ yields to pain and falls limp, broken and half-dead.

You and I cannot speak. Words are not needed. Look at him, look at him … slowly. After this … can you ever fear penance?

3. THE CROWNING WITH THORNS

Our King's eagerness for suffering has been fully satisfied! They lead my Lord to the courtyard of the palace, and there call together the whole troop (Mk 15: 16). The brutal soldiers strip his most pure body.

They drape a dirty purple rag about Jesus. They place a reed, as a scepter, in his right hand.

The crown of thorns, driven in by blows, makes him a mock king.... *Ave, Rex Iudæorum:* "Hail, King of the Jews!" (Mk 15: 18). And with their blows they wound his head. And they strike him . . . and spit on him.

Crowned with thorns and clothed in rags of purple, Jesus is shown to the Jewish crowd. *Ecce Homo:* "Here is the man!" And again the chief priests and their attendants raise the cry, saying, "Crucify him! Crucify him!" (Jn 19: 5-6).

You and I . . . haven't we crowned him anew with thorns and struck him and spat on him?

Never again, Jesus, never again.... And a firm and practical resolution marks the end of these ten Hail Marys.

4. THE CARRYING OF THE CROSS

Carrying his cross, Jesus goes out of the city to the place of the skulls — called Golgotha in Hebrew (Jn 19: 17). And they lay hold of a certain Simon from Cyrene, who is coming in from the country; and they make him take the cross and carry it behind Jesus (Lk 23: 26).

The prophecy of Isaiah (53: 12) is being fulfilled — *cum sceleratis reputatus est* ("he was counted among the wicked") — for two others are being led out with him to be put to death (Lk 23: 32).

If anyone would follow me.... Little friend, we are sad, living the Passion of our Lord Jesus. See how lovingly he embraces the cross. Learn from him. Jesus carries the cross for you: You... carry it for Jesus.

But don't drag the cross....Carry it squarely on your shoulder, because your cross, if you carry it so, will not be just any cross.... It will be the holy cross. Don't carry your cross with resignation: resignation is not a generous word. Love the cross. When you really love it, your cross will be... a Cross without a cross.

And, surely, you will find Mary on the way, just as Jesus did.

5. THE CRUCIFIXION AND DEATH OF OUR LORD

For Jesus of Nazareth, King of the Jews, the throne of triumph is ready. You and I do not see him writhe on being nailed. Suffering all that can be suffered, he spreads his arms in the ges-  ture of an Eternal Priest....

The soldiers take his holy garments and divide them into four parts. In order not to tear the tunic, they cast lots to decide whose it shall be. And so, once more, the words of Scripture are fulfilled: "They parted my garments among them, and for my clothes they cast lots' (Jn 19: 23–24).

Now he is on high....And close to her Son, at the foot of the cross, stand Mary... and Mary, the wife of Cleophas, and Mary Magdalene. And John, the disciple Jesus loved. *Ecce Mater tua:* "Behold your mother": he gives us his mother to be ours.

Earlier, they had offered him wine mixed with vinegar, and, when he had tasted it, he would not drink it (Mt 27: 34).

Now, he thirsts... for love, for souls. *Consummatum est:* "It is accomplished" (Jn 19: 30). Foolish child, look: All this... He has suffered it all for you. ... And for me. Can you keep from crying?

GLORIOUS MYSTERIES

1. THE RESURRECTION

When the Sabbath was over, Mary of Magdala and Mary, the mother of James, and Salome, bought spices with which to anoint the dead

body of Jesus. It is very early on the following day; just as the sun is rising, they come to the tomb (Mk 16: 1–2). And upon entering it they are dismayed, for they cannot find the body of our Lord. A youth, clothed in white, says to them: "Do not be afraid. I know that you seek Jesus of Nazareth. *Non est hic, surrexit enim sicut dixit:* He is not here; for he has risen, as he said" (Mt 28: 5).

He has risen! Jesus has risen: he is not in the tomb. Life has overcome death.

He appears to his most holy mother. He appears to Mary Magdalene, who is carried away by love. And to Peter and the rest of the apostles. And to you and me, who are his disciples and more in love than Mary Magdalene. The things we say to him! May we never die through sin; may our spiritual resurrection be eternal. And, before the decade is over, you kiss the wounds in his feet … and I, more daring—because I am more a child—place my lips upon his open side.

2. THE ASCENSION

Now the Master is teaching his disciples: he has opened their minds to understand the Scriptures, and he appoints them witnesses of his life and his miracles, of his passion and death, and of the glory of his resurrection (Lk 24: 45, 48). Then he brings them out as far as the outskirts of Bethany and blesses them. And as he does so, he withdraws from them and is carried up to heaven (Lk 24: 51) until a cloud takes him out of sight (Acts 1: 9).

Jesus has gone to the Father. Two angels in white approach us and say, "Men of Galilee, why do you stand looking up to heaven?" (Acts 1: 11). Peter and the others go back to Jerusalem *cum gaudio magno:* "with great joy" (Lk 24: 52). It is fitting that the sacred humanity of Christ should receive the homage, praise, and adoration of all the hierarchies of the angels and of all the legions of the blessed in heaven. But you and I feel like orphans: we are sad, and we go to Mary for consolation.

3. THE DESCENT OF THE HOLY SPIRIT

Our Lord had said: "I shall ask the Father, and he will give you another Advocate, another Consoler, to be with you for ever" (Jn 14: 16). The

disciples are gathered together in one room, when suddenly they hear what sounds like a powerful wind from heaven, the noise of which fills the entire house where they are assembled. At the same time something appears that seems like tongues of fire; these separate and come to rest on the head of each of them (Acts 2: 1-3).

The apostles are so filled with the Holy Spirit that they seem to be drunk (Acts 2: 13).

Then Peter stands up with the Eleven and addresses the people in a loud voice. We, people from a hundred nations, hear him. Each of us hears him in his own language—you and I in ours. He speaks to us of Christ Jesus and of the Holy Spirit and of the Father.

Peter is neither stoned nor thrown into prison. Of those who have heard him, three thousand are converted and baptized.

You and I, after helping the apostles administer Baptism, bless God the Father for his Son Jesus, and we, too, feel drunk with the Holy Spirit.

4. THE ASSUMPTION

Assumpta est Maria in cælum: gaudent angeli. God has taken Mary, body and soul, to heaven; and the angels rejoice!

So sings the Church. And so, with that same cry of joy, we begin our contemplation in this decade of the Holy Rosary.

The Mother of God has fallen asleep. Around her bed are the twelve apostles (Matthias in the place of Judas).

And we also, through a grace respected by all, are at her side.

But Jesus wants to have his mother, body and soul, in heaven. And the heavenly court, arrayed in all its splendor, greets our Lady. You and I—children, after all—take the train of Mary's magnificent blue cloak, and thus we are able to watch the marvelous scene.

The most blessed Trinity receives and showers honors on the Daughter, Mother and Spouse of God.... And so great is the Lady's majesty that the angels exclaim: Who is she?

5. THE CORONATION OF THE BLESSED VIRGIN

You are completely fair, and without blemish. You are a garden enclosed, my sister, my Bride, an enclosed garden, a sealed fountain. "*Veni, coronaberis*': "Come, you shall be crowned" (Sg 4: 7, 12, 8).

If you and I had been able, we too would have made her Queen and Lady of all creation.

"A great sign appeared in heaven: a woman with a crown of twelve stars upon her head, adorned with the sun and the moon at her feet" (Rev 12: 1). Mary, Virgin without stain, has made up for the fall of Eve; she has crushed the head of hell's serpent with her immaculate heel. Daughter of God, Mother of God, Spouse of God.

The Father, the Son, and the Holy Spirit crown her as the rightful Empress of the Universe.

And the angels pay her homage as her subjects ... and the patriarchs and prophets and apostles ... and the martyrs and confessors and virgins and all the saints . . . and all sinners, including you and me.

SALVE REGINA

Salve, Regína, mater misericórdiæ;
vita, dulcédo, et spes nostra, salve.
Ad te clamámus, éxsules fílii Evæ.
Ad te suspirámus, geméntes et flentes
in hac lacrimárum valle.
Eia ergo, advocáta nostra,
illos tuos misericórdes óculos
ad nos convérte.
Et Iesum, benedíctum fructum ventris tui,
nobis post hoc exsílium osténde.
O clemens, O pia, O dulcis Virgo María.

℣. Ora pro nobis, sancta Dei Génetrix.
℟. **Ut digni efficiámur promissiónibus Christi.**
Oremus.

Omnípotens sempitérne Deus, qui gloriósæ Vírginis Matris
Maríæ corpus et ánimam, ut dignum Fílii tui habitáculum éffici
mererétur, Spíritu Sancto cooperánte, præparásti: da, ut cuius
commemoratióne lætámur, eius pia intercessióne, ab instántibus
malis et a morte perpétua liberémur.
Per eúndem Christum Dóminum nostrum.

℟. **Amen.**
℣. Divínum auxílium máneat semper nobíscum.
℟. **Amen.**

HAIL HOLY QUEEN

This prayer has three parts. In the first part, the soul greets the Mother of God, invoking her mercy. In the second, the soul repeats the greeting and, in the name of all people, calls to holy Mary, whom we beg to look upon us with eyes of mercy and to love us with her son, Jesus. In the third, the soul proclaims the greatest and most fundamental title (epithet) of its intercessor—that is, Mother of God.

Hail, holy Queen, Mother of mercy,
our life, our sweetness, and our hope.
To you do we cry,
poor banished children of Eve.
To you do we send up our sighs,
mourning and weeping in this valley of tears.
Turn then, most gracious advocate,
your eyes of mercy toward us,
and after this our exile
show unto us the blessed fruit of your womb, Jesus.
O clement, O loving, O sweet Virgin Mary.

℣. Pray for us, O holy Mother of God.

℟. **That we may be made worthy of the promises of Christ.**

Let us pray.

Almighty and everlasting God, by the cooperation of the Holy Spirit you prepared the body and soul of Mary, glorious Virgin and Mother, to become the worthy habitation of your Son; grant that by her gracious intercession, in whose commemoration we rejoice, we may be delivered from present evils and from everlasting death. Through the same Christ our Lord.

℟. **Amen.**

℣. May the divine assistance remain with us always.

℟. **Amen.**

THE MEMORARE

The Memorare, a prayer attributed to St. Bernard of Clairvaux, is one of the best prayers expressing our confidence in the Blessed Virgin Mary.

Remember, O most gracious Virgin Mary, that never was it known that anyone who fled to your protection, implored your help, or sought your intercession was left unaided. Inspired with this confidence, I fly unto you, O Virgin of virgins, my Mother. To you I come, before you I stand, sinful and sorrowful. O Mother of the Word incarnate, despise not my petitions, but in your mercy hear and answer me. Amen.

LOVING MOTHER OF THE REDEEMER

Attr. to Hermann the Lame

Loving Mother of the Redeemer,
gate of heaven, star of the sea,
assist your people who have fallen, as we strive to rise again.
To the wonderment of nature, you bore your Creator,
yet remained a virgin after as before.
You who received Gabriel's joyful greeting,
have pity on us poor sinners.

HAIL, O QUEEN OF HEAVEN

Hail, O Queen of Heaven enthroned!
Hail, by angels mistress owned,
Root of Jesse! Hail the Gate!
Whence the world's true light was born:

Glorious Virgin, joy to thee,
Loveliest whom in heaven they see.
Fairest thou where all are fair!
Plead with Christ our sins to spare.

CANTICLE OF MARY (MAGNIFICAT)

To adore God is to acknowledge, in respect and absolute submission, the "nothingness of the creature" who would not exist but for God. To adore God is to praise and exalt him and to humble oneself, as Mary did in the Magnificat, confessing with gratitude that he has done great things and holy is his name (cf. Lk 1:46–49). The worship of the one God sets man free from turning in on himself, from the slavery of sin and the idolatry of the world. (CCC 2097)

The *Canticle of Mary* is recited at Evening Prayer in the Liturgy of the Hours.

My soul proclaims the greatness of the Lord, *
my spirit rejoices in God my Savior,

for he has looked with favor on his lowly servant. *
From this day all generations will call me blessed:

the Almighty has done great things for me, *
and holy is his Name.

He has mercy on those who fear him *
in every generation.

He has shown the strength of his arm, *
he has scattered the proud in their conceit.

He has cast down the mighty from their thrones, *
and has lifted up the lowly.

He has filled the hungry with good things, *
and the rich he has sent away empty.

He has come to the help of his servant Israel *
for he has remembered his promise of mercy,

the promise he made to our fathers, *
to Abraham and his children for ever.

AT THE CROSS HER STATION KEEPING
(STABAT MATER)

Sequence of Our Lady of Sorrows

Stabat Mater dolorósa
Iuxta crucem lacrimósa,
Dum pendébat Fílius.

At the cross, her station keeping,
stood the mournful mother
weeping, close to Jesus to the
last.

Cuius ánimam geméntem,
Contristátam et doléntem,
Pertransívit gládius.

Through her heart, his sorrow
sharing, all his bitter anguish
bearing, now at length the
sword had passed.

O quam tristis et afflícta
Fuit illa Benedícta
Mater Unigéniti!

Oh, how sad and sore distressed
was that mother highly blessed
of the sole begotten One!

Quæ mærébat, et dolébat,
Pia Mater, dum vidébat
Nati pœnas ínclyti.

Christ above in torment hangs,
she beneath beholds the pangs
of her dying, glorious Son.

Quis est homo, qui non fleret,
Matrem Christi si vidéret
In tanto supplício?

Is there one who would not
weep, whelmed in miseries so
deep, Christ's dear mother to
behold?

Quis non posset contristári,
Christi Matrem contemplári
Doléntem cum Fílio?

Can the human heart refrain
from partaking in her pain, in
that mother's pain untold?

Pro peccátis suæ gentis
Vidit Iesum in torméntis,
Et flagéllis súbditum.

Bruised, derided, cursed, defiled,
she beheld her tender Child, all
with bloody scourges rent.

Vidit suum dulcem natum
Moriéndo desolátum,
Dum emísit spíritum.

For the sins of his own nation
saw him hang in desolation till
his spirit forth he sent.

Eia Mater, fons amóris,
Me sentíre vim dolóris
Fac, ut tecum lúgeam.

O sweet mother! font of love,
touch my spirit from above,
make my heart with yours
accord.

Fac, ut árdeat cor meum
In amándo Christum Deum,
Ut sibi compláceam.

Make me feel as you have felt;
make my soul to glow and melt
with the love of Christ, my Lord.

Sancta Mater, istud agas,
Crucifíxi fige plagas
Cordi meo válide.

Holy mother, pierce me through,
in my heart each wound renew
of my Savior crucified.

Tui nati vulneráti,
Tam dignáti pro me pati,
Pœnas mecum dívide.

Let me share with you his pain,
who for all our sins was slain,
who for me in torments died.

Fac me tecum pie flere, Crucifíxo
condolére,
Donec ego víxero.

Let me mingle tears with you,
mourning him who mourned for
me, all the days that I may live .

Iuxta crucem tecum stare, Et me
tibi sociáre
In planctu desídero.

By the cross with you to stay,
there with you to weep and
pray, is all I ask of you to give.

Virgo vírginum præclára,
Mihi iam non sis amára:
Fac me tecum plángere.

Virgin of all virgins blest! Listen
to my fond request: let me share
your grief divine.

Fac, ut portem Christi mortem,
Passiónis fac consórtem,
Et plagas recólere.

Let me to my latest breath, in
my body bear the death of that
dying Son of yours.

Fac me plagis vulnerári,
Fac me cruce inebriári,
Et cruóre Fílii.

Wounded with his every wound,
steep my soul till it has swooned
in his very Blood away.

Flammis urar ne succénsus,
Per te, Virgo, sim defénsus
In die iudícii.

Be to me, O Virgin, nigh, lest
in flames I burn and die, in his
awful judgment day.

Christe, cum sit hinc exíre,
Da per Matrem me veníre
Ad palmam victóriæ.

Christ, when you shall call
me hence, be your mother
my defense, be your cross my
victory.

Quando corpus moriétur,
Fac, ut ánimæ donétur
Paradísi glória. Amen.
(T.P. Allelúia.)

While my body here decays, may
my soul your goodness praise,
safe in heaven eternally. Amen.
(Easter Time Alleluia.)

CONSECRATION TO THE BLESSED VIRGIN MARY

My Queen and my Mother, I give myself entirely to you and, in proof of my affection, I give you my eyes, my ears, my tongue, my heart, my whole being without reserve. Since I am your own, keep me and guard me as your property and possession. Amen.

BLESSED BE YOUR PURITY

Purity is an eminently positive virtue, which gains the grace of God for the person who lives it. It is the virtue of the beautiful and spotless soul. It elevates us to things divine. These ten verses praise Mary. Conceived without sin, she was always pure and brighter than snow.

Blessed be your purity,
May it be blessed for ever,
For no less than God takes delight
In such exalted beauty.
To you, heavenly Princess,
Holy Virgin Mary,
I offer on this day
My whole heart, life, and soul.
Look upon me with compassion;
Do not leave me, my mother.

PRAYER TO OUR LADY OF GUADALUPE

St. John Paul II

In January 1979, as his first of a long series of pastoral visits, Pope St. John Paul II went to Puebla, Mexico for the Conference of Latin American Bishops. During this trip, he visited the shrine of Our Lady of Guadalupe in the new basilica built in her honor. There, in the presence of those bishops, the Holy Father addressed this prayer to the Blessed Virgin Mary.

O Immaculate Virgin, mother of the true God and mother of the Church! You, who from this place revealed your clemency and your pity to all those who ask for your protection, hear the prayer that we address to you with filial trust, and present it to your Son Jesus, our sole Redeemer.

Mother of mercy, teacher of hidden and silent sacrifice, to you, who come to meet us sinners, we dedicate on this day all our being and all our love. We also dedicate to you our life, our work, our joys, our infirmities, and our sorrows.

Grant peace, justice, and prosperity to our peoples, for we entrust to your care all that we have and all that we are, our Lady and Mother.

We wish to be entirely yours and to walk with you along the way of complete faithfulness to Jesus Christ in his Church: hold us always with your loving hand.

Virgin of Guadalupe, Mother of the Americas, we pray to you for all the bishops, that they may lead the faithful along paths of intense Christian life, of love and humble service of God and souls.

Contemplate this immense harvest, and intercede with the Lord that he may instill a hunger for holiness in the whole People of God and grant abundant vocations of priests and religious, strong in the faith and zealous dispensers of God's mysteries.

Gain for our homes the grace of loving and respecting life in its beginnings with the same love with which you conceived in your womb the life of the Son of God. Blessed Virgin Mary, Mother of Fair Love, protect our families, so that they may always be united, and bless the upbringing of our children.

Our hope, look upon us with compassion, teach us to go continually to Jesus, and if we fall, help us to rise again, to return to him, by means of the confession of our faults and sins in the sacrament of Penance, which gives peace to the soul. We beg you to grant us a great love for all the holy sacraments, which are, as it were, the signs that your Son left us on earth.

Thus, most holy Mother, with the peace of God in our conscience, with our hearts free from evil and hatred, we will be able to bring to all true joy and true peace, which come to us from your Son, our Lord Jesus Christ, who, with God the Father and the Holy Spirit, lives and reigns for ever and ever. Amen.

MONTH OF MARY
(May Devotions)

*"God wills that all his gifts should come
to us through Mary"* (St. Bernard)

It was in Rome, towards the end of the eighteenth century, one fine evening in May. A child of the poor gathered his companions around him and led them to a statue of Mary, before which a lamp was burning, as is the custom in that holy city. There, these fresh young voices sang the Litany of our Lady. The next day, the little group, followed by other children, again gathered at the feet of the Mother of God. Next came their mothers, to join the little assembly. Soon, other groups were formed, and the devotion rapidly became popular. Holy souls, troubled by the disorderly conduct which always increases and becomes graver at the return of the pleasant springtime, saw in these growing practices the hand of God, and they cooperated with the designs of Providence by approving and promoting this new devotion, as a public and solemn act of reparation. The Month of Mary was founded.[5]

"This is the month in which, in the churches and individual homes, the most affectionate and fervent homage of prayers and devotions from the hearts of Christians is raised to Mary. It is also the month in which from his throne descend upon us the most generous and abundant gifts of the Divine Mercy."[6]

In our own times, we Catholics, wanting to be close to her always, offer her special presents in May: pilgrimages, visits to churches dedicated to her, little sacrifices in her honor, periods of study and well-finished work offered up to her, and a more attentive recitation of the rosary.

May 1

MARY: THE MOTHER OF GOD

"When the Blessed Virgin said yes, freely, to the plans revealed to her by the Creator, the divine Word assumed a human nature—a rational soul and a body—which was formed in the most pure womb of Mary. The divine nature and the human were united in a single Person: Jesus Christ, true God and, thenceforth, true man; the only-begotten and eternal Son of the Father and from that moment on,

---

5. Cf. A Carthusian, *A Month with Mary*, London: Burns and Oates, 1950.
6. Paul VI, *The Month of Mary*, 1967.

as man, the true Son of Mary. This is why Our Lady is the mother of the Incarnate Word, of the second Person of the Blessed Trinity, who has united our human nature to himself for ever, without any confusion of the two natures. The greatest praise we can give to the Blessed Virgin is to address her loud and clear by the name that expresses her very highest dignity: 'Mother of God'."[7]

Let us offer to our Mother today:
Brief but frequent prayers of love, such as:
"Mother of God, your petitions are most powerful."

May 2

MARY: THE MOST PERFECT CREATURE

"She who is full of grace, the object of God's pleasure, exalted above all the angels and the saints, lived an ordinary life.

"Mary is as much a creature as we are, with a heart like ours, made for joy and mirth as well as suffering and tears. Before Gabriel communicates to her God's plan, our Lady does not know that she has been chosen from all eternity to be the mother of the Messiah. She sees herself as a lowly creature. That is why she can acknowledge, with full humility, that 'he who is mighty has done great things' for her."[8]

Let us offer to our Mother today:
Many glances of affection and many words of love,
when we see her image or picture in our home,
in the church, or anywhere.

May 3

MARY AND THE BLESSED TRINITY

"Through the Incarnation of our Lord in her immaculate womb, Mary, the Daughter of God the Father, is also the Spouse of God the Holy Spirit and the Mother of God the Son."[9]

Let us offer to our Mother today:
A "Hail Mary" each time the clock strikes another hour.

---

7. This excerpt and the following thirty excerpts are taken from homilies of Saint Josemaria Escriva in *Christ Is Passing By* and *Friends of God*. This one is from "Mother of God and Our Mother," FG 274.

8. "Cause of Our Joy," CPB 172.

May 4

MARY'S FAMILY: THE TRINITY ON EARTH

"It is only natural that the Church rejoice as it contemplates the modest home of Jesus, Mary, and Joseph. We read in the hymn from Matins on the feast of the holy Family: 'It is pleasing to recall the humble house of Nazareth and its slender resources. It is pleasing to tell again in song Jesus' hidden life. Jesus grows up in hidden seclusion, to be trained in Joseph's unpretentious trade. The loving mother sits beside her dear Son, the good wife by her husband, content if her loving attention can ease and comfort them in their weariness.'"[10]

Let us offer to our Mother today:
A loving review of her life with Jesus,
as we recite the Joyful Mysteries of the Rosary.

May 5

MARY: HER IMMACULATE CONCEPTION

"How would we have acted, if we could have chosen our own mother? I'm sure we would have chosen the one we have, adorning her with every possible grace. That is what Christ did. Christ being all-powerful, all-wise, Love itself, his power carried out his Will. . . . This is the clearest reason why our Lord granted his mother , from the very moment of her Immaculate Conception, all possible privileges. She was free from the power of Satan. She is beautiful, spotless and pure in soul and body."[11]

Let us offer to our Mother today:
The renewal of our baptismal vows.

---

9. "Mother of God and Our Mother," FG 274.

10. "Marriage: A Christian Vocation," CPB 22.

11. "Cause of Our Joy," CPB 171.

May 6

THE ANNUNCIATION MARY: THE FIRST TABERNACLE

"If you seek Mary, you will find Jesus. And you will learn a bit more about what is in the heart of God, who humbles himself, discarding all manifestations of his power and majesty to take the form of a servant. Speaking in human terms, we could say that God outdoes himself, because he goes much further than he needs to go in order to save us. The only way to measure what he does is to say that it cannot be measured; it comes from a madness of love which leads him to take on our flesh and bear the weight of our sins."[12]

Let us offer to our Mother today:
*The Angelus recited punctually
at noon and with great affection.*

May 7

MARY: OUR MODEL IN ORDINARY LIFE

"We can't forget that Mary spent nearly every day of her life just like millions of other women who look after their families, bring up their children, and take care of their houses. Mary sanctifies the ordinary, everyday things—what some people wrongly regard as unimportant and insignificant: everyday work, looking after those closest to you, visits to friends and relatives. What a blessed ordinariness, that can be so full of love of God."[13]

Let us offer to our Mother today:
*Affectionate details of service
and attention to those closest to us.*

---

12. "To Jesus through Mary," CPB 144.
13. "To Jesus through Mary," CPB 148.

May 8

MARY: MOTHER OF CHRIST

"Iesus Christus, Deus homo: Jesus Christ, God-man. This is one of the 'mighty works of God,' which we should reflect upon and thank him for. He has come to bring 'peace on earth to men of good will,' to all who want to unite their wills to the holy will of God—not just the rich, not just the poor, but everyone: all the brethren. We are all brothers in Jesus, children of God, brothers of Christ. His mother is our mother."[14]

Let us offer to our Mother today:
Jesus himself, when we receive him in holy Communion.

May 9

MARY: WELCOMING THE SHEPHERDS

"You must look at the Child in the manger. He is our Love. Look at him, realizing that the whole thing is a mystery. We need to accept this mystery on faith and use our faith to explore it very deeply. To do this, we must have the humble attitude of a Christian soul."[15]

Let us offer to our Mother today:
Small hidden sacrifices,
especially those that go against the grain.

May 10

MARY: PRESENTING JESUS IN THE TEMPLE

"She teaches us to have charity. Remember the scene of the presentation of Jesus in the temple. An old man, Simeon, said to Mary, 'Behold: This child is destined to bring about the fall of many and the rise of many in Israel—and to be a sign, which people will refuse to acknowledge, so that the thoughts of many hearts shall be made manifest. As for your own soul, it shall have a sword pierce it.' So great is Mary's love for all mankind that she, too, fulfilled Christ's

---

14. "Christ Triumphs through Humility," CPB 13.
15. "Christ Triumphs through Humility," CPB 13.

words: 'Greater love has no man than this, that he should lay down his life for his friends.'"[16]

Let us offer to our Mother today:
A pilgrimage to one of her shrines.

May 11

MARY: WELCOMING THE MAGI

"'Going into the house, they saw the child with Mary, his mother .' Our Lady is always near her Son. The Magi are not received by a king on a high throne, but by a child in the arms of his Mother. Let us ask the Mother of God, who is our mother, to prepare for us the way that leads to the fullness of love. . . . Her sweet heart knows the surest path for finding Christ."[17]

Let us offer to our Mother today:
*A visit to a poor person to communicate
our Lady's concern for that person.*

May 12

MARY: HER FLIGHT TO EGYPT
WITH JOSEPH AND THE CHILD JESUS

"The mystery of Mary helps us to see that in order to approach God, we must become little. Christ said to his disciples: 'Believe me, unless you become like little children again, you shall not enter the kingdom of heaven.'

"To become children, we must renounce our pride and self-sufficiency, recognizing that we can do nothing by ourselves. We must realize that we need grace and the help of God our Father to find our way and keep to it."[18]

Let us offer to our Mother today:
*A visit to a lonely person to share
the joy of trusting in God alone.*

---

16. "Mother of God and Our Mother," FG 287.
17. "The Epiphany of Our Lord," CPB 38.
18. "To Jesus through Mary," CPB 143.

May 13

MARY: HER HIDDEN LIFE WITH JESUS

"I like to go back in my imagination to the years Jesus spent close to his Mother, years which span almost the whole of his life on earth. I like to picture him as a little child, cared for by Mary, who kisses him and plays with him. I like to see him growing up before the loving eyes of his Mother and of Joseph, his father on earth. What tenderness and care Mary and the Holy Patriarch must have shown towards Jesus, as they looked after him during his childhood, all the while, silently, learning so much from him. Their souls would become more and more like the soul of that Son, who was both Man and God. This is why his Mother, and after her St. Joseph, understand better than anyone the feelings of the Heart of Christ; and the two of them are thus the best way, I would say the only way, to reach the Savior."[19]

Let us offer to our Mother today:
*The effort of doing our ordinary work well,
on time, with competence and finesse.*

May 14

MARY: LOSING AND FINDING THE CHILD JESUS

"The Mother of God, who looked for her Son so anxiously when he was lost (through no fault of her own) and experienced such great joy in finding him, will help us retrace our steps and put right whatever may be necessary when, because of our carelessness or our sins, we have been unable to recognize Christ. With her help, we will know the happiness of holding him in our arms once more and telling him we will never lose him again."[20]

Let us offer to our Mother today:
*A good, sincere, sorrowful confession
of our sins and failures, in the sacrament of Penance.*

---

19. "Mother of God and Our Mother," FG 281.
20. "Mother of God and Our Mother," FG 278.

May 15

MARY: AT CANA

"In his Gospel, St. John has recorded a wonderful phrase of our Lady. At the wedding of Cana she turned to the waiters and said: 'Do whatever he tells you.' That is what it is all about—getting people to face Jesus and ask him: 'Lord, what do you want me to do?'"[21]

Let us offer to our Mother today:
*Prompt obedience, when we are called or asked
to do some errand or some act of service.*

May 16

MARY: AT THE FOOT OF THE CROSS

"We find her on Calvary, at the foot of the cross, praying. This is nothing new for Mary. She has always acted like this, in fulfilling her duties and looking after her home. As she went about the things of this earth, she kept her attention on God."[22]

Let us offer to our Mother today:
*An act of contrition, said many times, asking her
to offer our sorrow for our sins to Jesus crucified.*

May 17

MARY: THE SORROWING MOTHER

"Our Lady is there listening to the words of her Son, united to him in his suffering, when he cried out 'My God, my God, why have you forsaken me?' What could she do? She united herself fully with the redemptive love of her Son and offered to the Father her immense sorrow, which pierced her pure heart like a sharp-edged sword."[23]

Let us offer to our Mother today:
*The mortification of keeping quiet about any pain
or discomfort, any inconvenience or disappointment,
uniting it with her pain as she stood by her crucified Son.*

---

21. "To Jesus through Mary," CPB 149.
22. "A Life of Prayer," FG 241.
23. "Mother of God and Our Mother," FG 288.

May 18

MARY: THE CO-REDEMPTRIX

"It is with good reason that the popes have called Mary Co-Redemptrix. 'So fully, in union with her suffering and dying Son, did she suffer and nearly die; so fully, for the sake of the salvation of all souls, did she abdicate the rights of a mother over her Son, and immolate him, insofar as it was in her power, to satisfy the justice of God, that it can rightly be said that she redeemed mankind together with Christ.' This gives us a deeper understanding of that moment in the Passion of our Lord, which we shall never tire of meditating: Stabat autem iuxta crucem Iesu mater eius, 'There, standing by the cross of Jesus, was his mother.'"[24]

Let us offer to our Mother today:
Five small hidden sacrifices
in honor of the five major wounds of our Lord.

May 19

MARY: HER FAITH

"If our faith is weak, we should turn to Mary. St. John tells us that it was because of the miracle that Christ performed, at his mother's request, at the marriage feast at Cana, that 'his disciples learned to believe in him.' Our Mother is always interceding with her Son, so that he may attend to our needs and show himself to us in such a way that we can cry out, 'You are the Son of God!'"[25]

Let us offer to our Mother today:
The "Memorare" for the person in our family
who most needs the help of our Lady.

May 20

MARY: OUR HOPE

"Our Lady, a full participant in the work of our salvation, follows in the footsteps of her Son: the poverty of Bethlehem, the everyday work of a hidden life in Nazareth, the manifestation of his divinity in

---

24. "Mother of God and Our Mother," FG 287.
25. "Mother of God and Our Mother," FG 285.

Cana of Galilee, the tortures of his passion, the divine sacrifice on the cross, the eternal blessedness of paradise.

"All of this affects us directly, because this supernatural itinerary is the way we are to follow. Mary shows us that we can walk this path with confidence. She has preceded us on the way of imitating Christ; her glorification is the firm hope of our own salvation. For these reasons we call her 'our hope, cause of our joy.'"[26]

Let us offer to our Mother today:
A smile when we do not feel like smiling.

May 21
MARY'S PRAYER

"Let us ask the Blessed Virgin to make us contemplatives, to teach us to recognize the constant calls from God at the door of our heart. Let us ask her now: Our Mother, you brought to earth Jesus, who reveals the love of our Father God. Help us to recognize him in the midst of the cares of each day. Stir up our mind and will so that we may listen to the voice of God, to the calls of grace."[27]

Let us offer to our Mother today:
A visit to Jesus truly present in the Blessed Sacrament.

May 22
MARY: EVER VIRGIN

"The purity, humility, and generosity of Mary are in sharp contrast to our wretchedness and selfishness. To the extent that we realize this, we should feel moved to imitate her. We too are creatures of God, and if we strive to imitate her fidelity, God will surely do great things in us. Our small worth is no obstacle, because God chooses what is of little value so that the power of his love may be more manifest."[28]

Let us offer to our Mother today:
The prayer "Blessed be your purity," (p. 176).

---

26. "Cause of Our Joy," CPB 176.
27. "Cause of Our Joy," CPB 174.
28. "Cause of Our Joy," CPB 172.

May 23

MARY: QUEEN OF THE APOSTLES

"If we take our Lady's hand, she will make us realize more fully that all men are our brothers—because we are all sons of that God whose daughter, spouse, and mother she is. Our neighbors' problems must be our problems. Christian fraternity should be something very deep in the soul, so that we are indifferent to no one. Mary, who brought up Jesus and accompanied him through his life and is now beside him in heaven, will help us recognize Jesus as he crosses our path and makes himself present to us in the needs of others."[29]

Let us offer to our Mother today:
*A kind word, a friendly conversation,
a helping hand to persons with whom we live or work.*

May 24

MARY: HELP OF CHRISTIANS

"Yes, we are still pilgrims, but our Mother has gone on ahead, where she points to the reward for our efforts. She tells us that we can make it. If we are faithful, we will reach home. Not only is the Blessed Virgin our model, but she is also the Help of Christians. And as we besiege her with our petitions—'Show that you are our Mother'—she cannot help but watch over her children with motherly care."[30]

Let us offer to our Mother today:
*In addition to the mysteries of the day,
one more part (five decades) of the Holy Rosary.*

May 25

MARY: OUR MOTHER

"Find out for yourself by personal experience the meaning of Mary's maternal love. It is not enough just to know that she is our Mother, and to think and talk about her as such. She is your Mother and you are her child. She loves you as if you were her only child in this world.

---

29. "To Jesus through Mary," CPB 145.
30. "Cause of our Joy," CPB 177.

Treat her accordingly. Tell her about everything that happens to you; honor her and love her. No one will do it for you or as well as you."[31]

Let us offer to our Mother today:
*Many affectionate thoughts and prayers, by saying,
"Mary, my mother," each time we pause in our work.*

May 26
MARY: THE WAY TO JESUS

"Mary does the immense favor of bringing to the cross, of placing face to face with the example of the Son of God, those who come close to her and contemplate her life. It is in this confrontation that Christian life is decided. And here Mary intercedes for us so that our behavior may lead to a reconciliation of the younger brother—you and me—with the firstborn Son of the Father.

"Many conversions, many decisions to give oneself to the service of God have been preceded by an encounter with Mary. Our Lady has encouraged us to look for God, to desire to change, to lead a new life."[32]

Let us offer to our Mother today:
Teaching someone how to say the Holy Rosary.

May 27
MARY: MOTHER OF FAIR LOVE

"This is what explains Mary's life—her love. A complete love, so complete that she forgets herself and is happy just to be there where God wants her, fulfilling with care what God wants her to do. That is why even her slightest action is never routine or vain but, rather, full of meaning. Mary, our Mother, is for us both an example and a way. In the ordinary circumstances in which God wants us to live, we have to try to be like her."[33]

Let us offer to our Mother today:
*The resolution to say, before going to sleep every night,
three Hail Marys.*

---

31. "Mother of God and our Mother," FG 293.

32. "To Jesus through Mary," CPB 149.

33. "To Jesus through Mary," CPB 148.

May 28

THE ASSUMPTION MARY: TAKEN UP TO HEAVEN

"Mary has gone to heaven in both body and soul, and the angels rejoice. I can imagine, too, the delight of St. Joseph, her most chaste spouse, who awaited her in paradise. Yet what of us who remain on earth? Our faith tells us that here below, in our present life, we are pilgrims, wayfarers. Our lot is one of suffering, of sacrifices, and privations. Nonetheless, joy must mark the rhythm of our steps. 'Serve the Lord with joy'—there is no other way to serve him."[34]

Let us offer to our Mother today:
A smile when someone corrects us or misjudges us.

May 29

MARY: THE QUEEN OF HEAVEN

"She lives now and is protecting us. She is there [in heaven], body and soul, with the Father and the Son and the Holy Spirit. She is the same person who was born in Palestine, who gave herself to God while still a child, who received the message from St. Gabriel the Archangel, who gave birth to our Savior, and who stood beside him at the foot of the Cross. In her, all ideals become a reality. But we should never think that this sublime greatness of hers makes her inaccessible to us. She is the one who is full of grace and the sum of all perfections . . . and she is also our Mother."[35]

Let us offer to our Mother today:
The "Hail Holy Queen" at each hour.

---

34. "Cause of our Joy," CPB 177.
35. "Mother of God and Our Mother," FG 292.

May 30

MARY: THE CHANNEL OF GRACE

"Her power before God is such that she can obtain anything that we ask for, and, like any mother, she wants to answer our prayers. Like any mother, also, she knows and understands our weaknesses. She encourages us and makes excuses for us. She makes the way easy for us, and even when we think there is no possible solution for our worry, she always has one ready to offer us."[36]

Let us offer to our Mother today:
A visit or a conversation with a friend or relative
whom we want to encourage to go to Confession.

May 31

THE VISITATION MARY SINGS OF THE LOVE OF GOD

"God is interested in even the smallest events in the lives of his creatures—in your affairs and mine—and he calls each of us by name. This certainty that the faith gives enables us to look at everything in a new light. And everything, while remaining exactly the same, becomes different, because it is an expression of God's love. Our life is turned into a continuous prayer, we find ourselves with good humor and a peace that never ends, and everything we do is an act of thanksgiving running through all our day. 'My soul magnifies the Lord,' Mary sang, 'and my spirit rejoices in God, my Savior.'"[37]

Let us offer to our Mother today:
The Holy Rosary said with concentration and affection.

---

36. "Mother of God and Our Mother," FG 292.
37. "To Jesus through Mary," CPB 144.

NOVENA TO THE IMMACULATE CONCEPTION

Pope Bl. Pius IX proclaimed the dogma of the Immaculate Conception on December 8, 1854: that she was conceived free from all stain of Original Sin. This feast has been celebrated since the eighth century.

FIRST DAY (NOVEMBER 30)

Mary, the new Eve

Introductory Prayer

Lord God, may our gifts be sanctified by the Holy Spirit,
who formed the Blessed Virgin Mary
to be a new creation
and sent down upon her
the dew of heavenly grace,
so that her womb might bear the fruit of our salvation,
Jesus Christ, your Son,
who lives and reigns for ever and ever. Amen.

Reading   Gn 3: 1-6, 13-15

The serpent was more subtle than any other wild creature that the Lord God had made. He said to the woman, "Did God say, 'You shall not eat of any tree of the garden'?" And the woman said to the serpent, "We may eat of the fruit of the trees of the garden; but God said, 'You shall not eat of the fruit of the tree which is in the midst of the garden; neither shall you touch it, lest you die.'"

But the serpent said to the woman, "You will not die. For God knows that when you eat of it your eyes will be opened, and you will be like God, knowing good and evil." So when the woman saw that the tree was good for food, and that it was a delight to the eyes, and that the tree was to be desired to make one wise, she took of its fruit and ate; and she also gave some to her husband, and he ate.

Then the Lord God said to the woman, "What is this that you have done?" The woman said, "The serpent beguiled me, and I ate." The Lord God said to the serpent,

"Because you have done this, / cursed are you above all cattle, / and above all wild animals; / upon your belly you shall go, / and dust you shall eat all the days of your life. / I will put enmity between you and the woman, / and between your seed and her seed; / he shall bruise your head, / and you shall bruise his heel."

Consideration

Mary, Mother of the Incarnate Word, is placed at *the very center of that enmity*, that struggle which accompanies the history of humanity on earth and the history of salvation itself. In this central place, she who belongs to the "weak and poor of the Lord" bears in herself, like no other member of the human race, that "glory of grace" which the Father "has bestowed on us in his beloved Son," and this *grace determines the extraordinary greatness and beauty* of her whole being. Mary thus remains before God, and also before the whole of humanity, as the unchangeable and inviolable sign of God's election, spoken in Paul's letter: "in Christ… he chose us… before the foundation of the world… he destined us… to be his sons' (Eph 1: 4, 5). This election is more powerful than any experience of evil and sin, than all that "enmity" which marks the history of man. In this history Mary remains a sign of sure hope.[38]

The Holy Rosary (pp. 149ff.) may be prayed.

Concluding Prayer

Lord God,
you prepared a worthy dwelling place for your Son
by the Immaculate Conception of the Virgin;
grant, we pray,
that, as you preserved her from all stain of sin
in your foreknowledge of his death,
so we, by her intercession,
may come to you with pure hearts.
We ask this through Christ our Lord. Amen.

---

38. RMat 11.

SECOND DAY (DECEMBER 1)

Mary, full of grace

Introductory Prayer

Father, in your plan for our salvation
your Word became man,
announced by an angel
and born of the Virgin Mary.
May we who believe
that she is the Mother of God
receive the help of her prayers.
We ask this through Christ our Lord. Amen.

Reading   Lk 1: 26–33

The angel Gabriel was sent from God to a city of Galilee named Nazareth, to a virgin betrothed to a man whose name was Joseph, of the house of David; and the virgin's name was Mary. And he came to her and said, "Hail, full of grace, the Lord is with you!" But she was greatly troubled at the saying, and considered in her mind what sort of greeting this might be.

And the angel said to her, "Do not be afraid, Mary, for you have found favor with God. And behold, you will conceive in your womb and bear a son, and you shall call his name Jesus. He will be great, and will be called the Son of the Most High; and the Lord God will give to him the throne of his father David, and he will reign over the house of Jacob for ever; and of his kingdom there will be no end."

Consideration

When we read that the messenger addresses Mary as "full of grace," the Gospel context, which mingles revelations and ancient promises, enables us to understand that among all the "spiritual blessings in Christ" this is a special "blessing." In the mystery of Christ she is *present* even "before the creation of the world," as the one whom the Father "has chosen" as *Mother* of his Son in the Incarnation. And, what is more, together with the Father, the Son has chosen her, entrusting her eternally to the Spirit of holiness. In an entirely special and exceptional way Mary is united to Christ, and similarly she is *eternally loved in this "beloved Son,"* this

Son who is of one being with the Father, in whom is concentrated all the "glory of grace." At the same time, she is and remains perfectly open to this 'gift from above' (cf. Jas 1: 17). As the Council teaches, Mary "stands out among the poor and humble of the Lord, who confidently await and receive salvation from him."[39]

The Holy Rosary (pp149ff.) may be prayed.

Concluding Prayer

Lord God, you prepared a worthy dwelling place for your Son
by the Immaculate Conception of the Virgin;
grant, we pray,
that, as you preserved her from all stain of sin
in your foreknowledge of his death,
so we, by her intercession,
may come to you with pure hearts.
We ask this through Christ our Lord. Amen.

THIRD DAY (DECEMBER 2)
Mary, the handmaid of the Lord

Introductory Prayer

Lord God, when your Son came down from heaven,
Mary had conceived him in her heart
before she conceived him in her womb:
grant that by holy and just deeds
we may show forth in our lives the Christ
whom we have received by faith,
and who lives and reigns with you and the Holy Spirit,
one God, for ever and ever. Amen.

Reading   Lk 1: 34–38

And Mary said to the angel, "How shall this be, since I have no husband?"

And the angel said to her, "The Holy Spirit will come upon you, and the power of the Most High will overshadow you; therefore the child to be born

---

39. RMat 8.

will be called holy, the Son of God. And behold, your kinswoman Elizabeth in her old age has also conceived a son; and this is the sixth month with her who was called barren. For with God nothing will be impossible."

And Mary said, "Behold, I am the handmaid of the Lord; let it be done to me according to your word." And the angel departed from her.

Consideration

Indeed, at the Annunciation Mary entrusted herself to God completely, with the "full submission of intellect and will," manifesting "the obedience of faith" to him who spoke to her through his messenger. She responded, therefore, *with all her human and feminine "I,"* and this response of faith included both perfect cooperation with "the grace of God that precedes and assists' and perfect openness to the action of the Holy Spirit, who "constantly brings faith to completion by his gifts."

The word of the living God, announced to Mary by the angel, referred to her: "And behold, you will conceive in your womb and bear a son" (Lk 1: 31). By accepting this announcement, Mary was to become the "Mother of the Lord," and the divine mystery of the Incarnation was to be accomplished in her: "The Father of mercies willed that the consent of the predestined Mother should precede the Incarnation." And Mary gives this consent, after she has heard everything the messenger has to say.... The mystery of the Incarnation was accomplished when Mary uttered her *fiat:* "Let it be to me according to your word," which made possible, as far as it depended upon her in the divine plan, the granting of her Son's desire.[40]

The Holy Rosary (pp. 149ff.) may be prayed.

Concluding Prayer

Lord God,
you prepared a worthy dwelling place for your Son
by the Immaculate Conception of the Virgin;
grant, we pray,
that, as you preserved her from all stain of sin
in your foreknowledge of his death,
so we, by her intercession,
may come to you with pure hearts.
We ask this through Christ our Lord. Amen.

40. RMat 13.

FOURTH DAY (DECEMBER 3)

Mary, blessed among women

Introductory Prayer

Lord, our God,
Savior of the human family,
you brought salvation and joy to the house of Elizabeth
through the visit of the Blessed Virgin Mary,
the Ark of the new Covenant.
We ask that, in obedience
to the inspiration of the Holy Spirit,
we too may bring Christ to others
and magnify your name by the praise of our lips
and the holiness of our lives.
We ask this through Christ our Lord. Amen.

Reading   Lk 1: 39–44

In those days Mary arose and went with haste into the hill country, to
a city of Judah, and she entered the house of Zechariah and greeted
Elizabeth. And when Elizabeth heard the greeting of Mary, the babe
leaped in her womb; and Elizabeth was filled with the Holy Spirit and
she exclaimed with a loud cry, "Blessed are you among women, and
blessed is the fruit of your womb! And why is this granted me, that the
mother of my Lord should come to me? For behold, when the voice of
your greeting came to my ears, the babe in my womb leaped for joy."

Consideration

Immediately after the narration of the Annunciation, the evangelist
Luke guides us in the footsteps of the Virgin of Nazareth towards "a
city of Judah" (Lk 1: 39). According to scholars, this city would be the
modern Ain Karim, situated in the mountains, not far from Jerusalem.
Mary arrived there "in haste," to visit Elizabeth her kinswoman....

Moved by charity, therefore, Mary goes to the house of her kinswoman. When Mary enters, Elizabeth replies to her greeting and
feels the child leap in her womb, and, being "filled with the Holy
Spirit" she *greets Mary* with a loud cry: "Blessed are you among
women, and blessed is the fruit of your womb!" (cf. Lk 1: 40–42).
Elizabeth's exclamation or acclamation was subsequently to become

part of the *Hail Mary*, as a continuation of the angel's greeting, thus
becoming one of the Church's most frequently used prayers. But still
more significant are the words of Elizabeth in the question which
follows: "And why is this granted me, that the mother of my Lord
should come to me?" (Lk 1: 43). Elizabeth bears witness to Mary:
she recognizes and proclaims that before her stands the mother of
the Lord, the mother of the Messiah. The son whom Elizabeth is
carrying in her womb also shares in this witness: "The babe in my
womb leaped for joy" (Lk 1: 44). This child is the future John the
Baptist, who at the Jordan will point out Jesus as the Messiah.[41]

The Holy Rosary (pp149ff.) may be prayed.

Concluding Prayer

Lord God, you prepared a worthy dwelling place for your Son
by the Immaculate Conception of the Virgin;
grant, we pray,
that, as you preserved her from all stain of sin
in your foreknowledge of his death,
so we, by her intercession,
may come to you with pure hearts.
We ask this through Christ our Lord. Amen.

FIFTH DAY (DECEMBER 4)

Mary, model of faith

Introductory Prayer

All-holy Father, eternal God,
in your goodness
you prepared a royal throne for your Wisdom
in the womb of the Blessed Virgin Mary;
bathe your Church in the radiance of your life-giving Word,
that it may press forward on its pilgrim way
in the light of your truth,
and so come to the joy
of a perfect knowledge of your love.

---

41. RMat 12.

God of wisdom,
in your desire to restore us to your friendship
after we had lost it by sin,
you chose the Blessed Virgin Mary
as the seat of your Wisdom.
Grant through her intercession
that we may seek not the folly of the wise
but the loving service
that marks out the poor in spirit.
We ask this through Christ our Lord. Amen.

Reading   Lk 1: 45–56

[Elizabeth exclaimed:]

"Blessed is she who believed that there would be a fulfillment of
what was spoken to her from the Lord."

And Mary said,
"My soul magnifies the Lord,
and my spirit rejoices in God my Savior,
for he has regarded the low estate of his handmaiden.

For behold, henceforth all generations
    will call me blessed;
for he who is mighty has done great things for me,
and holy is his name.
And his mercy is on those who fear him,
from generation to generation.

He has shown strength with his arm,
he has scattered the proud
    in the imagination of their hearts,
he has put down the mighty from their thrones
and exalted those of low degree;
he has filled the hungry with good things,
and the rich he has sent empty away.

He has helped his servant Israel,
in remembrance of his mercy,

as he spoke to our fathers,
to Abraham and to his posterity for ever."
And Mary remained with her about three months, and returned to her home.

Consideration

Elizabeth's words "And blessed is she who believed" do not apply only to that particular moment of the Annunciation. Certainly the Annunciation is the culminating moment of Mary's faith in her awaiting of Christ, but it is also the point of departure from which her whole "journey towards God" begins, her whole pilgrimage of faith. And on this road, in an eminent and truly heroic manner — indeed, with an ever greater heroism of faith — the "obedience" which she professes to the word of divine revelation will be fulfilled. Mary's "obedience of faith" during the whole of her pilgrimage will show surprising similarities to the faith of Abraham. Just like the Patriarch of the People of God, so too Mary, during the pilgrimage of her filial and maternal *fiat*, "in hope believed against hope."

In the expression "Blessed is she who believed," we can therefore rightly find *a kind of "key"* which unlocks for us the innermost reality of Mary, whom the angel hailed as "full of grace." If as "full of grace" she has been eternally present in the mystery of Christ, through faith she became a sharer in that mystery in every extension of her earthly journey. She "advanced in her pilgrimage of faith," and at the same time, in a discreet yet direct and effective way, she made present to humanity *the mystery of Christ*. And she still continues to do so. Through the mystery of Christ, she too is present within mankind. Thus through the mystery of the Son the mystery of the Mother also is made clear.[42]

The Holy Rosary (pp.149ff.) may be prayed.

Concluding Prayer

Lord God, you prepared a worthy dwelling place for your Son
by the Immaculate Conception of the Virgin;
grant, we pray,
that, as you preserved her from all stain of sin
in your foreknowledge of his death,
so we, by her intercession,

---

42. RMat 14, 19.

may come to you with pure hearts.
We ask this through Christ our Lord. Amen.

SIXTH DAY (DECEMBER 5)

Mary, co-redemptrix (sharer in the suffering of her Son)

Introductory Prayer

Lord our God, in your eternal wisdom
you fill out the Passion of Christ
through the suffering that his members endure
in the many trials of this life.
As you gave his mother strength in her agony
to stand by the cross of your Son,
grant that we too may bring loving comfort to others
in their distress of mind or body.
We ask this through Christ our Lord. Amen.

Reading   Lk 2: 25–35

Now there was a man in Jerusalem whose name was Simeon, and
this man was righteous and devout, looking for the consolation of
Israel, and the Holy Spirit was upon him. And it had been revealed
to him by the Holy Spirit that he should not see death before he had
seen the Lord's Christ. And inspired by the Spirit he came into the
Temple; and when the parents brought in the child Jesus, to do for
him according to the custom of the law, he took him up in his arms
and blessed God and said, "Lord, now lettest thou thy servant depart
in peace, according to thy word; for mine eyes have seen thy salvation which thou hast prepared in the presence of all peoples, a light
for revelation to the Gentiles, and for glory to thy people Israel."

And his father and his mother marveled at what was said about him;
and Simeon blessed them and said to Mary his mother, "Behold, this
child is set for the fall and rising of many in Israel, and for a sign that
is spoken against (and a sword will pierce through your own soul
also), that thoughts out of many hearts may be revealed."

Consideration

A just and God-fearing man, called Simeon, appears at this beginning of Mary's "journey" of faith. His words, suggested by the Holy Spirit (cf. Lk 2: 25–27), confirm the truth of the Annunciation. For we read that he took up in his arms the child to whom—in accordance with the angel's command—the name Jesus was given (cf. Lk 2: 21). Simeon's words match the meaning of this name, which is Savior: "God is salvation." Turning to the Lord, he says: "For my eyes have seen your *salvation* which you have prepared *in the presence of all peoples*, a light for revelation to the Gentiles, and for glory to your people Israel" (Lk 2: 30–32). At the same time, however, Simeon addresses Mary with the following words: "Behold, this child is set for the fall and rising of many in Israel, and for *a sign that is spoken against*, that thoughts out of many hearts may be revealed"; and he adds with direct reference to her: "and a sword will pierce through your own soul also" (Lk 2: 34–35).

Simeon's words cast new light on the announcement which Mary had heard from the angel: Jesus is the Savior, he is "a *light* for revelation" to mankind. Is not this what was manifested in a way on Christmas night, when the *shepherds* came to the stable (cf. Lk 2: 8–20)? Is not this what was to be manifested even more clearly in the coming of the *Magi from the East* (Mt 2: 1–12)? But at the same time, at the very beginning of his life, the Son of Mary, and his Mother with him, will experience in themselves the truth of those other words of Simeon: "a sign that is spoken against" (Lk 2: 34).

Simeon's words seem like a *second Annunciation to Mary*, for they tell her of the actual historical situation in which the Son is to accomplish his mission, namely, in misunderstanding and sorrow. While this announcement on the one hand confirms her faith in the accomplishment of the divine promises of salvation, on the other hand it also reveals to her that she will have to live her obedience of faith in suffering, at the side of the suffering Savior, and that her motherhood will be mysterious and sorrowful.[43]

The Holy Rosary (pp. 149ff.) may be prayed.

Concluding Prayer

Lord God,
you prepared a worthy dwelling place for your Son
by the Immaculate Conception of the Virgin;
grant, we pray,

---

43. RMat 16.

that, as you preserved her from all stain of sin
in your foreknowledge of his death,
so we, by her intercession,
may come to you with pure hearts.
We ask this through Christ our Lord. Amen.

SEVENTH DAY (DECEMBER 6)

*Mary, the first of those
who heard the word of God and did it*

Introductory Prayer

Lord our God, you sent your Son from heaven
into the womb of the Blessed Virgin
to be your saving Word and our Bread of Life:
grant that like Mary we may welcome Christ,
by treasuring his words in our hearts
and celebrating in faith
the deep mysteries of our redemption.
We ask this through Christ our Lord. Amen.

Reading   Lk 11: 27–28

As he said this, a woman in the crowd raised her voice and said to
him, "Blessed is the womb that bore you, and the breasts that you
sucked!" But he said, "Blessed, rather, are those who hear the word
of God and keep it!"

Consideration

The Gospel of Luke records the moment when "a woman in the
crowd raised her voice" and said to Jesus: *"Blessed is the womb that
bore you, and the breasts that you sucked! (Lk 11: 27).* These words
were an expression of praise of Mary as Jesus' mother according to
the flesh....

But to the blessing uttered by that woman upon her who was
his mother according to the flesh, Jesus replies in a significant
way: "Blessed, rather, are *those who hear the word of God and keep
it"* (Lk 11: 28). He wishes to divert attention from motherhood understood only as a fleshly bond, in order to direct it towards those

mysterious bonds of the spirit which develop from hearing and keeping God's word....

Without any doubt, Mary is worthy of blessing by the very fact that she became the mother of Jesus according to the flesh ("Blessed is the womb that bore you, and the breasts that you sucked"), but also and especially because already at the Annunciation she accepted the word of God, because she believed it, *because she was obedient to God*, and because she "kept" the word and "pondered it in her heart" (cf. Lk 1: 38, 45; 2: 19, 51) and by means of her whole life accomplished it. Thus we can say that the blessing proclaimed by Jesus is not in opposition, despite appearances, to the blessing uttered by the unknown woman, but rather coincides with that blessing in the person of this Virgin Mother, who called herself only "the handmaid of the Lord" (Lk 1: 38)....

If *through faith* Mary became the bearer of the Son given to her by the Father through the power of the Holy Spirit, while preserving her virginity intact, in that same faith she *discovered and accepted the other dimension of motherhood* revealed by Jesus during his messianic mission. One can say that this dimension of motherhood belonged to Mary from the beginning, that is to say from the moment of the conception and birth of her Son. From that time she was "the one who believed."... Thus *in a sense* Mary as mother became *the first "disciple" of her Son*, the first to whom he seemed to say "Follow me," even before he addressed this call to the apostles or to anyone else (cf. Jn 1: 43).[44]

The Holy Rosary (pp. 149ff.) may be prayed.

Concluding Prayer

Lord God,
you prepared a worthy dwelling place for your Son
by the Immaculate Conception of the Virgin;
grant, we pray,
that, as you preserved her from all stain of sin
in your foreknowledge of his death,
so we, by her intercession,
may come to you with pure hearts.
We ask this through Christ our Lord. Amen.

---

44. RMat 20.

EIGHTH DAY (DECEMBER 7)

Mary, mediatrix of graces

Introductory Prayer

God of heaven and earth,
your Son, Jesus the Lord,
while dying on the altar of the cross,
chose Mary, his mother, to be our mother also.
Grant that we,
who entrust ourselves to her maternal care,
may always be protected
when we call upon her name.
We ask this through Christ our Lord. Amen.

Reading   Jn 2: 1–11

On the third day there was a marriage at Cana in Galilee, and the mother of Jesus was there; Jesus also was invited to the marriage, with his disciples. When the wine failed, the mother of Jesus said to him, "They have no wine." And Jesus said to her, "O woman, what have you to do with me? My hour has not yet come." His mother said to the servants, "Do whatever he tells you."

Now six stone jars were standing there, for the Jewish rites of purification, each holding twenty or thirty gallons. Jesus said to them, "Fill the jars with water." And they filled them up to the brim. He said to them, "Now draw some out, and take it to the steward of the feast." So they took it.

When the steward of the feast tasted the water now become wine, and did not know where it came from (though the servants who had drawn the water knew), the steward of the feast called the bridegroom and said to him, "Every man serves the good wine first; and when men have drunk freely, then the poor wine; but you have kept the good wine until now." This, the first of his signs, Jesus did at Cana in Galilee, and manifested his glory; and his disciples believed in him.

Consideration

Mary is present at Cana in Galilee as the *Mother of Jesus*, and in a significant way she *contributes* to that "beginning of the signs" which reveal the messianic power of her Son. We read: "When the wine gave out, the mother of Jesus said to him, 'They have no wine.' And Jesus said to her, 'O woman, what have you to do with me? My hour has not yet come'" (Jn 2: 3–4). In John's Gospel that "hour" means the time appointed by the Father when the Son accomplishes his task and is to be glorified (cf. Jn 7: 30; 8: 20; 12: 23, 27; 13: 1; 17: 1; 19: 27). Even though Jesus' reply to his mother sounds like a refusal (especially if we consider the blunt statement "My hour has not yet come," rather than the question), Mary nevertheless turns to the servants and says to them: "Do whatever he tells you" (Jn 2: 5). Then Jesus orders the servants to fill the stone jars with water, and the water becomes wine, better than the wine which has previously been served to the wedding guests.[45]

In this passage of John's Gospel we find as it were a first manifestation of the truth concerning Mary's maternal care. This truth has also found expression *in the teaching of the Second Vatican Council....* "Mary's maternal function towards mankind in no way obscures or diminishes the unique mediation of Christ, but rather shows its efficacy," because ""there is one mediator between God and men, the man Christ Jesus"" (1 Tm 2: 5).... The episode at Cana in Galilee offers us *a sort of first announcement of Mary's mediation,* wholly oriented towards Christ and tending to the revelation of his salvific power.

From the *text of John* it is evident that it is a mediation which is maternal. As the Council proclaims: Mary became "a mother to us in the order of grace." This motherhood in the order of grace flows from her divine motherhood. Because she was, by the design of divine Providence, the mother who nourished the divine Redeemer, Mary became "an associate of unique nobility, and the Lord's humble handmaid," who "cooperated by her obedience, faith, hope, and burning charity in the Savior's work of restoring supernatural life to souls." And "this *maternity of Mary in the order of grace*... will last without interruption until the eternal fulfillment of all the elect."[46]

The Holy Rosary (pp. 149ff.) may be prayed.

---

45. RMat 21.
46. RMat 22.

Concluding Prayer

Lord God,
you prepared a worthy dwelling place for your Son
by the Immaculate Conception of the Virgin;
grant, we pray,
that, as you preserved her from all stain of sin
in your foreknowledge of his death,
so we, by her intercession,
may come to you with pure hearts.
We ask this through Christ our Lord. Amen.

NINTH DAY (DECEMBER 8)

Mary, Mother of God and our mother

Introductory Prayer

God of mercies,
your only Son, while hanging on the cross,
appointed Mary, his mother,
to be our mother also.
Like her, and under her loving care,
may your Church grow day by day,
rejoice in the holiness of its children,
and so attract to itself all the peoples of the earth.
We ask this through Christ our Lord. Amen.

Reading   Jn 19: 23–27

When the soldiers had crucified Jesus they took his garments and
made four parts, one for each soldier; also his tunic. But the tunic was
without seam, woven from top to bottom; so they said to one another, "Let us not tear it, but cast lots for it to see whose it shall be." This
was to fulfill the scripture, "They parted my garments among them,
and for my clothing they cast lots." So the soldiers did this.

But standing by the cross of Jesus were his mother, and his mother's
sister, Mary the wife of Clopas, and Mary Magdalene. When Jesus
saw his mother, and the disciple whom he loved standing near, he
said to his mother, "Woman, behold, your son!" Then he said to the

disciple, "Behold, your mother!" And from that hour the disciple took her to his own home.

Consideration

> If John's description of the event at Cana presents Mary's caring motherhood at the beginning of Christ's messianic activity, another passage from the same Gospel confirms this motherhood in the salvific economy of grace at its crowning moment, namely when Christ's sacrifice on the cross, his paschal mystery, is accomplished. John's description is concise: *'Standing by the cross of Jesus* were his mother, and his mother's sister, Mary the wife of Clopas, and Mary Magdalene. When Jesus saw his mother, and the disciple whom he loved standing near, he said to his mother: "Woman, behold your son!" Then he said to the disciple, "Behold your mother!" And from that hour the disciple took her into his own home' (Jn 19: 25–27)....

> And yet the 'testament of Christ's Cross' says more. Jesus highlights a new relationship between Mother and Son, the whole truth and reality of which he solemnly confirms. One can say that if Mary's motherhood of the human race had already been outlined, now it is clearly stated and established. It *emerges* from the definitive accomplishment of *the Redeemer's paschal mystery*. The mother of Christ, who stands at the very center of this mystery—a mystery which embraces each individual and all humanity—is given as mother to every single individual and all mankind.[47]

The Holy Rosary (pp. 149ff) may be prayed.

Concluding Prayer

Lord God,
you prepared a worthy dwelling place for your Son
by the Immaculate Conception of the Virgin;
grant, we pray,
that, as you preserved her from all stain of sin
in your foreknowledge of his death,
so we, by her intercession,
may come to you with pure hearts.
We ask this through Christ our Lord. Amen.

---

47. RMat 23.

DEVOTIONS TO ST. JOSEPH

God chose Joseph to be the husband of the Virgin Mary and the foster father of Jesus; he is considered the second greatest saint. He took an active part in the divine plan of redemption, as an example of humility and faith. Scripture tells us also that he was just, pure, gentle, prudent, and unfailingly obedient to the divine will. Joseph worked as an artisan and carried out his work for the glory of God—sanctifying his profession. According to tradition, he died in the presence of Jesus and Mary. We wish to imitate him by renewing our desire to be faithful. We know that the only meaning of our life is to be faithful to the Lord till the very end, as was Joseph. Pope Bl. Pius IX named him Patron of the Universal Church, and Pope Bl. John XXIII included his name in the Roman Canon (Eucharistic Prayer I).

What must Joseph have been, how grace must have worked through him, that he should have been able to fulfill this task of the human upbringing of the Son of God!

For Jesus must have resembled Joseph: in his way of working, in the features of his character, in his way of speaking. Jesus' realism, his eye for detail, the way he sat at table and broke bread, his preference for using everyday situations to give doctrine—all this reflects his childhood and the influence of Joseph.

It is not possible to ignore this sublime mystery: Jesus, who is man, who speaks with the accent of a particular district of Israel, who resembles a carpenter called Joseph, is the Son of God.[1]

SEVEN SUNDAYS DEVOTION

Joseph shared the happiness—but also the sufferings—of Mary. The Seven Sundays Devotion honors the seven joys and sorrows of St. Joseph. It starts on the seventh Sunday previous to March 19 (the last Sunday of January or the first Sunday of February).

---

1. CPB 55.

FIRST SUNDAY

His sorrow when he decided to leave the
Blessed Virgin; his joy when the angel told
him the mystery of the Incarnation.

Introductory Prayer

O chaste spouse of Mary,
great was the trouble and anguish of your heart
when you were considering
quietly sending away your inviolate spouse;
yet your joy was unspeakable
when the surpassing mystery of the Incarnation
was made known to you by the angel.
By this sorrow and this joy,
we beseech you to comfort our souls,
both now and in the sorrows of our final hour,
with the joy of a good life and a holy death
after the pattern of your own life
and death in the arms of Jesus and Mary.

Reading   Mt 1: 18–25

Now the birth of Jesus Christ took place in this way. When his mother Mary had been betrothed to Joseph, before they came together she was found to be with child of the Holy Spirit; and her husband Joseph, being a just man and unwilling to put her to shame, resolved to send her away quietly.

But as he considered this, behold, an angel of the Lord appeared to him in a dream, saying, "Joseph, son of David, do not fear to take Mary, your wife, for that which is conceived in her is of the Holy Spirit; she will bear a son, and you shall call his name Jesus, for he will save his people from their sins."

All this took place to fulfill what the Lord had spoken by the prophet: "Behold, a virgin shall conceive and bear a son, and his name shall be called Emmanuel" (which means, God with us).

When Joseph woke from sleep, he did as the angel of the Lord commanded him; he took his wife, but knew her not until she had borne a son; and he called his name Jesus.

Consideration

In the course of that pilgrimage of faith which was his life, Joseph, like Mary, remained faithful to God's call until the end. While Mary's life was the bringing to fullness of that *fiat* first spoken at the Annunciation, *at the moment of Joseph's own "annunciation"* he said nothing; instead he simply "*did* as the angel of the Lord commanded him" (Mt 1: 24). And *this first "doing" became the beginning of "Joseph's way."*[2]

In the words of the "annunciation" by night, Joseph not only heard the divine truth concerning his wife's indescribable vocation; he *also heard once again the truth about his own vocation.* This "just" man, who, in the spirit of the noblest traditions of the Chosen People, loved the Virgin of Nazareth and was bound to her by a husband's love, was once again called by God to this love.

"Joseph did as the angel of the Lord commanded him; he took his wife" into his home (Mt 1: 24); what was conceived in Mary was "of the Holy Spirit." From expressions such as these, are we not to suppose that his *love as a man was also given new birth by the Holy Spirit?* Are we not to think that the love of God which has been poured forth into the human heart through the Holy Spirit (cf. Rom 5: 5) molds every human love to perfection?[3]

Through his complete self-sacrifice, Joseph expressed his generous love for the Mother of God, and gave her a husband's "gift of self." Even though he decided to draw back so as not to interfere in the plan of God which was coming to pass in Mary, Joseph obeyed the explicit command of the angel and took Mary into his home, while respecting the fact that she belonged exclusively to God.[4]

Here the Litany of St. Joseph (pp. 224f.) may be prayed.

Concluding Prayer

℣. Pray for us, blessed Joseph,

℟. **That we may be made worthy of the promises of Christ.**
Let us pray.
Almighty God,
in your infinite wisdom and love
you chose Joseph to be the husband of Mary,

---

2. RC 17.
3. RC 19.
4. RC 20.

the mother of your Son.
As we enjoy his protection on earth,
may we have the help of his prayers in Heaven.
We ask this through Christ our Lord. Amen.

SECOND SUNDAY

His sorrow when he saw Jesus born in poverty;
his joy when the angels announced Jesus' birth.

Introductory Prayer

O most blessed patriarch, glorious Saint Joseph,
who were chosen to be the foster father
    of the Word made flesh,
your sorrow at seeing the child Jesus born in such poverty
was suddenly changed into heavenly exultation
when you heard the angelic hymn
and beheld the glories of that resplendent night.
By this sorrow and this joy,
we implore you to obtain for us
the grace to pass over from life's pathway
to hear angelic songs of praise
and to rejoice in the shining splendor of celestial glory.

Reading   Lk 2: 1–20

In those days a decree went out from Caesar Augustus that all
the world should be enrolled. This was the first enrollment, when
Quirinius was governor of Syria. And all went to be enrolled, each to
his own city. And Joseph also went up from Galilee, from the city of
Nazareth, to Judaea, to the city of David, which is called Bethlehem,
because he was of the house and lineage of David, to be enrolled
with Mary, his betrothed, who was with child. And while they were
there, the time came for her to be delivered. And she gave birth to
her firstborn son and wrapped him in swaddling cloths, and laid him
in a manger, because there was no place for them in the inn.

And in that region there were shepherds out in the field, keeping
watch over their flock by night. And an angel of the Lord appeared to

them, and the glory of the Lord shone around them, and they were filled with fear.

And the angel said to them, "Be not afraid; for behold, I bring you good news of a great joy which will come to all the people; for to you is born this day in the city of David a Savior, who is Christ the Lord. And this will be a sign for you: you will find a babe wrapped in swaddling cloths and lying in a manger." And suddenly there was with the angel a multitude of the heavenly host praising God and saying, "Glory to God in the highest, and on earth peace among men with whom he is pleased!"

When the angels went away from them into heaven, the shepherds said to one another, "Let us go over to Bethlehem and see this thing that has happened, which the Lord has made known to us." And they went with haste, and found Mary and Joseph, and the babe lying in a manger. And when they saw it they made known the saying which had been told them concerning this child; and all who heard it wondered at what the shepherds told them. But Mary kept all these things, pondering them in her heart. And the shepherds returned, glorifying and praising God for all they had heard and seen, as it had been told them.

Consideration

Journeying to Bethlehem for the census in obedience to the orders of legitimate authority, Joseph fulfilled for the child the significant task of officially inserting the name "Jesus, son of Joseph of Nazareth" (cf. Jn 1: 45) in the registry of the Roman Empire. This registration clearly shows that Jesus belongs to the human race as a man among men, a citizen of this world, subject to laws and civil institutions, but also *"Savior of the world."*[5]

As guardian of the mystery "hidden for ages in the mind of God," which begins to unfold before his eyes "in the fullness of time," *Joseph, together with Mary,* is a privileged witness to the birth of the Son of God into the world *on Christmas night in Bethlehem....*

Joseph was an eyewitness to this birth, which took place in conditions that, humanly speaking, were embarrassing—a first announcement of that "self-emptying" (cf. Phil 2: 5-8) which Christ freely accepted for the forgiveness of sins. Joseph also *witnessed the adoration of the shepherds* who arrived at Jesus' birthplace after the angel had brought

---

5. RC 9.

them the great and happy news (cf. Lk 2: 15-16). Later he also *witnessed the homage of the magi who came from the East* (cf. Mt 2: 11).[6]

Here the Litany of St. Joseph (pp. 224f.) may be prayed.

Concluding Prayer

℣. Pray for us, blessed Joseph,

℟. **That we may be made worthy of the promises of Christ.**
Let us pray.
Almighty God,
in your infinite wisdom and love
you chose Joseph to be the husband of Mary,
the mother of your Son.
As we enjoy his protection on earth,
may we have the help of his prayers in Heaven.
We ask this through Christ our Lord. Amen.

THIRD SUNDAY

His sorrow when he saw Jesus' Blood shed in circumcision;
his joy in giving him the name Jesus.

Introductory Prayer

O glorious Saint Joseph,
who faithfully obeyed the law of God,
your heart was pierced
at the sight of the most precious blood
that was shed by the infant Savior during his circumcision,
but the name of Jesus gave you new life
and filled you with quiet joy.
By this sorrow and this joy,
obtain for us the grace
to be freed from all sin during life and to die rejoicing,
with the holy name of Jesus in our hearts and on our lips.

---

6. RC 10.

Reading
Lk 2: 21

And at the end of eight days, when he was circumcised, he was called Jesus, the name given by the angel before he was conceived in the womb.

Consideration

A son's circumcision was the first religious obligation of a father, and with this ceremony (cf. Lk 2: 21) Joseph exercised his right and duty with regard to Jesus.

The principle which holds that all the rites of the Old Testament are a shadow of the reality (cf. Heb 9: 9f.; 10: 1) serves to explain why Jesus would accept them. As with all the other rites, circumcision too is "fulfilled" in Jesus. God's covenant with Abraham, of which circumcision was the sign (cf. Gn 17: 13), reaches its full effect and perfect realization in Jesus, who is the "yes" of all the ancient promises (cf. 2 Cor 1: 20).[7]

At the circumcision Joseph names the child "Jesus." This is the only name in which there is salvation (cf. Acts 4: 12). Its significance had been revealed to Joseph at the moment of his "annunciation": "You shall call the child Jesus, for he will save his people from their sins" (cf. Mt 1: 21). In conferring the name, Joseph declares his own legal fatherhood over Jesus, and in speaking the name he proclaims the child's mission as Savior.[8]

Here the Litany of St. Joseph (pp. 224f.) may be prayed.

Concluding Prayer

℣. Pray for us, blessed Joseph,

℟. **That we may be made worthy of the promises of Christ.**

Let us pray.
Almighty God,
in your infinite wisdom and love
you chose Joseph to be the husband of Mary,
the mother of your Son.
As we enjoy his protection on earth,

---

7. RC 11
8. RC 12.

may we have the help of his prayers in Heaven.
We ask this through Christ our Lord. Amen.

FOURTH SUNDAY

His sorrow when he heard the prophecy of Simeon;
his joy when he learned that many would be
saved through the sufferings of Jesus.

Introductory Prayer

O most faithful Saint Joseph,
who shared the mysteries of our redemption,
the prophecy of Simeon,
touching the sufferings of Jesus and Mary,
caused you to shudder with mortal dread
but at the same time filled you with a blessed joy
for the salvation and glorious resurrection
that would be attained by countless souls.
By this sorrow and this joy,
obtain for us that we may be
of the number of those who,
through the merits of Jesus
and the intercession of Mary the Virgin Mother,
are predestined to a glorious resurrection.

Reading   Lk 2: 22–35

And when the time came for their purification according to the law
of Moses, they brought him up to Jerusalem to present him to the
Lord (as it is written in the law of the Lord, "Every male that opens
the womb shall be called holy to the Lord") and to offer a sacrifice
according to what is said in the law of the Lord, "a pair of turtle-
doves, or two young pigeons."

Now there was a man in Jerusalem, whose name was Simeon, and
this man was righteous and devout, looking for the consolation of
Israel, and the Holy Spirit was upon him. And it had been revealed
to him by the Holy Spirit that he should not see death before he had
seen the Lord's Christ. And inspired by the Spirit he came into the
Temple; and when the parents brought in the child Jesus, to do for

him according to the custom of the law, he took him up in his arms and blessed God and said,

"Lord, now lettest thou thy servant depart in peace,
according to thy word;
for mine eyes have seen thy salvation
which thou hast prepared in the presence of all peoples,
a light for revelation to the Gentiles,
and for glory to thy people Israel."

And his father and his mother marveled at what was said about him; and Simeon blessed them and said to Mary his mother, "Behold, this child is set for the fall and rising of many in Israel, and for a sign that is spoken against (and a sword will pierce through your own soul also), that thoughts out of many hearts may be revealed."

Consideration

This rite, to which Luke refers (2: 22ff.), includes the ransom of the firstborn and sheds light on the subsequent stay of Jesus in the Temple at the age of twelve.

The *ransoming of the firstborn* is another obligation of the father, and it is fulfilled by Joseph. Represented in the firstborn is the people of the covenant, ransomed from slavery in order to belong to God. Here, too, Jesus—who is the true "price" of ransom (cf. 1 Cor 6: 20; 7: 23; 1 Pt 1: 19)—not only "fulfills" the Old Testament rite, but at the same time transcends it, since he is not a subject to be redeemed, but the very author of redemption.

The gospel writer notes that "his father and his mother marveled at what was said about him" (Lk 2: 23), in particular at *what Simeon said* in his canticle to God, when he referred to Jesus as the "salvation which you have prepared in the presence of all peoples, a light for revelation to the Gentiles, and for glory to your people Israel" and as a "sign that is spoken against" (cf. Lk 2: 30–34).[9]

In the words of the Council: "It pleased God, in his goodness and wisdom, to reveal himself and to make known the mystery of his will (cf. Eph 1: 9). His will was that men should have access to the Father, through Christ, the Word made flesh, in the Holy Spirit, and become sharers in the divine nature" (cf. Eph 2: 18; 2 Pt 1: 4).[10]

---

9. RC 13.
10. DV 2.

Together with Mary, Joseph is the first guardian of this divine mystery.
Together with Mary, and in relation to Mary, he shares in this final
phase of God's self-revelation in Christ, and he does so from the very
beginning.[11]

Here the **Litany of St. Joseph** (pp. 224f.) may be prayed.

Concluding Prayer

℣. Pray for us, blessed Joseph,

℟. **That we may be made worthy of the promises of Christ.**
Let us pray.
Almighty God,
in your infinite wisdom and love
you chose Joseph to be the husband of Mary,
the mother of your Son.
As we enjoy his protection on earth,
may we have the help of his prayers in Heaven.
We ask this through Christ our Lord. Amen.

FIFTH SUNDAY

His sorrow when he had to flee to Egypt;
his joy in being always with Jesus and Mary.

Introductory Prayer

O most watchful guardian of the Son of God,
glorious Saint Joseph,
great was your toil in supporting
and waiting upon the Son of God,
especially during the flight into Egypt!
Yet, how you rejoiced
to have God himself always near you.
By this sorrow and this joy,
obtain for us the grace that would keep us safe from the devil,
especially the help we need to flee from dangerous situations.
May we serve Jesus and Mary,
and for them alone may we live and happily die.

---

11. RC 5.

Reading   Mt 2: 13–15

Now when they had departed, behold, an angel of the Lord appeared
to Joseph in a dream and said, "Rise, take the child and his mother,
and flee to Egypt, and remain there till I tell you; for Herod is about
to search for the child, to destroy him." And he rose and took the
child and his mother by night, and departed to Egypt, and remained
there until the death of Herod. This was to fulfill what the Lord had
spoken by the prophet, "Out of Egypt have I called my son."

Consideration

Herod learned from the magi, who came from the East, about the
birth of the "king of the Jews" (Mt 2: 2). And when the magi departed, he "sent and killed all the male children in Bethlehem and
in all that region who were two years old or under" (Mt 2: 16). By
killing them all, he wished to kill the newborn "king of the Jews"
whom he had heard about.[12]

The Church deeply venerates this Family and proposes it as the
model of all families. Inserted directly in the mystery of the Incarnation, the Family of Nazareth has its own special mystery. And in this
mystery, as in the Incarnation, one finds a true fatherhood: *the human form of the family of the Son of God,* a true human family,
formed by the divine mystery. *In this family, Joseph is the father: his fatherhood*
is not one that derives from begetting offspring; but neither is
it an "apparent" or merely "substitute" fatherhood. Rather, it is one
that *fully shares in authentic human fatherhood* and the mission of a
father in the family. This is a consequence of the hypostatic union:
humanity taken up into the unity of the Divine Person of the Word–
Son, Jesus Christ. Together with human nature, *all that is human, and
especially the family*—as the first dimension of man's existence in
the world—*is also taken up* in Christ. Within this context, Joseph's
human fatherhood was also "taken up" in the mystery of Christ's
Incarnation.[13]

Here the Litany of St. Joseph (pp. 224f.) may be prayed.

Concluding Prayer

℣. Pray for us, blessed Joseph,

℟. **That we may be made worthy of the promises of Christ.**

---

12. RC 14.
13. RC 21.

Let us pray.
Almighty God,
in your infinite wisdom and love
you chose Joseph to be the husband of Mary,
the mother of your Son.
As we enjoy his protection on earth,
may we have the help of his prayers in Heaven.
We ask this through Christ our Lord. Amen.

SIXTH SUNDAY

His sorrow when he was afraid to return to his homeland;
his joy on being told by the angel to go to Nazareth.

Introductory Prayer

O glorious Saint Joseph,
you marveled to see the King of Heaven
obedient to your commands.
Your consolation in bringing Jesus out of the land of Egypt
was troubled by your fear of Archelaus.
Nevertheless, being assured by an angel,
you lived in gladness at Nazareth with Jesus and Mary.
By this sorrow and this joy,
obtain for us that our hearts
may be delivered from harmful fears,
so that we may rejoice in peace of conscience
and may live with Jesus and Mary,
and, like you, may die in their company.

Reading   Mt 2: 19–23; Lk 2: 40

When Herod died, behold, an angel of the Lord appeared in a dream
to Joseph in Egypt, saying, "Rise, take the child and his mother, and
go to the land of Israel, for those who sought the child's life are
dead." And he rose and took the child and his mother, and went to
the land of Israel. But when he heard that Archelaus reigned over
Judaea in place of his father Herod, he was afraid to go there, and
being warned in a dream he withdrew to the district of Galilee. And

he went and dwelt in a city called Nazareth, that what was spoken by the prophets might be fulfilled, "He shall be called a Nazarene." And the child grew and became strong, filled with wisdom; and the favor of God was upon him.

Consideration

Work was the daily expression of love in the life of the Family of Nazareth. The Gospel specifies the kind of work Joseph did in order to support his family: he was a carpenter. This simple word sums up Joseph's entire life. For Jesus, these were hidden years, the years to which Luke refers after recounting the episode that occurred in the Temple: "And he went down with them and came to Nazareth, and was obedient to them" (Lk 2: 51). This *"submission"* or obedience of Jesus in the house of Nazareth should be *understood as a sharing in the work of Joseph.* Having learned the work of his presumed father, he was known as "the carpenter's son." If the Family of Nazareth is an example and model for human families, in the order of salvation and holiness, so too, by analogy, is Jesus' work at the side of Joseph the carpenter. In our own day, the Church has emphasized this by instituting the liturgical memorial of St. Joseph the Worker on May 1. *Human work,* and especially manual labor, *receives special prominence in the Gospel.* Along with the humanity of the Son of God, work too has been taken up in the mystery of the Incarnation, *and has also been redeemed in a special way.* At the workbench where he plied his trade together with Jesus, Joseph brought human work closer to the mystery of the Redemption.[14]

In the human growth of Jesus "in wisdom, age, and grace," the *virtue of industriousness* played a notable role, since "work is a human good" which "transforms nature" and makes man "in a sense, more human."[15]

What is crucially important here is the sanctification of daily life, a sanctification which each person must acquire according to his or her own state, and one which can be promoted according to a model accessible to all people: "St. Joseph is the model of those humble ones that Christianity raises up to great destinies; ... he is the proof that in order to be a good and genuine follower of Christ, there is no need of great things—it is enough to have the common, simple, and human virtues, but they must be true and authentic."[16]

---

14. RC 22.
15. RC 23.
16. RC 24.

Here the **Litany of St. Joseph** (pp.224f.) may be prayed.

Concluding Prayer

℣. Pray for us, blessed Joseph,

℟. **That we may be made worthy of the promises of Christ.**
Let us pray.
Almighty God, in your infinite wisdom and love
you chose Joseph to be the husband of Mary,
the mother of your Son.
As we enjoy his protection on earth,
may we have the help of his prayers in Heaven.
We ask this through Christ our Lord. Amen.

SEVENTH SUNDAY

His sorrow when he lost the child Jesus;
his joy in finding him in the Temple.

Introductory Prayer

O glorious Saint Joseph,
pattern of all holiness,
when you lost the child Jesus,
you sought him sorrowing for the space of three days,
until with great joy you found him again in the Temple,
sitting in the midst of the doctors.
By this sorrow and this joy,
we ask you, with our hearts upon our lips,
to keep us from ever having the misfortune
of losing Jesus through mortal sin.
Grant also that we always may seek him with unceasing sorrow,
when we commit a serious sin,
until we find him again,
ready to show us his great mercy
in the sacrament of Reconciliation.

Reading

Lk 2: 41–50

Now his parents went to Jerusalem every year at the feast of the Passover. And when he was twelve years old, they went up according to custom; and when the feast was ended, as they were returning, the boy Jesus stayed behind in Jerusalem. His parents did not know it, but, supposing him to be in the company, they went a day's journey, and they sought him among their kinsfolk and acquaintances; and when they did not find him, they returned to Jerusalem, seeking him.

After three days they found him in the Temple, sitting among the teachers, listening to them and asking them questions; and all who heard him were amazed at his understanding and his answers. And when they saw him they were astonished; and his mother said to him, "Son, why have you treated us so? Behold, your father and I have been looking for you anxiously."

And he said to them, "How is it that you sought me? Did you not know that I must be in my Father's house?" And they did not understand the saying which he spoke to them.

Consideration

Joseph, of whom Mary had just used the words "your father," heard this answer. That, after all, is what all the people said and thought: Jesus was "the son (as was supposed) of Joseph" (Lk 3: 23). Nonetheless, the reply of Jesus in the Temple brought once again to the mind of his "presumed father" what he had heard on that night twelve years earlier: "Joseph … do not fear to take Mary as your wife, for *that which is conceived in her is of the Holy Spirit*." From that time onwards he knew that he was a guardian of the mystery of God, and it was *precisely this mystery* that the twelve-year-old *Jesus brought to mind*: "I must be in my Father's house."[17]

Here the Litany of St. Joseph (pp. 224f.) may be prayed.

Concluding Prayer

℣. Pray for us, blessed Joseph,

℟. **That we may be made worthy of the promises of Christ.**

---

17. RC 15.

Let us pray.
Almighty God,
in your infinite wisdom and love
you chose Joseph to be the husband of Mary,
the mother of your Son.
As we enjoy his protection on earth,
may we have the help of his prayers in Heaven.
We ask this through Christ our Lord. Amen.

LITANY OF ST. JOSEPH

Lord, have mercy.	**Lord, have mercy.**
Christ, have mercy.	**Christ, have mercy.**
Holy Trinity, one God.	**Have mercy on us.**
Holy Mary,	**pray for us.**
Saint Joseph,…	
Noble son of the House of David,…	
Light of patriarchs,…	
Husband of the Mother of God,…	
Guardian of the Virgin,…	
Foster father of the Son of God,…	
Faithful guardian of Christ,…	
Head of the Holy Family,…	
Joseph, chaste and just,…	
Joseph, prudent and brave,…	
Joseph, obedient and loyal,…	
Pattern of patience,…	
Lover of poverty,…	
Model of workers,…	
Example to parents,…	
Guardian of virgins,…	
Pillar of family life,…	
Comfort of the troubled,…	
Hope of the sick,…	
Patron of the dying,…	

Terror of evil spirits,

Protector of the Church,...
pray for us.

Lamb of God, you take away
    the sins of the world.
Spare us, O Lord.

Lamb of God, you take away
    the sins of the world.
Graciously hear us, O Lord.

Lamb of God, you take away
    the sins of the world.
Have mercy on us.

℣. God made him master of his household.

℟. **And put him in charge of all that he owned.**

Let us pray.

Almighty God,

in your infinite wisdom and love

you chose Joseph to be the husband of Mary,

the mother of your Son.

As we enjoy his protection on earth,

may we have the help of his prayers in Heaven.

We ask this through Christ our Lord.

℟. **Amen.**

VARIOUS PRAYERS

PERSONAL MEDITATION

Before

My Lord and my God, I firmly believe that you are here, that you see me, that you hear me. I adore you with profound reverence; I ask your pardon for my sins and the grace to make this time of prayer fruitful. My immaculate Mother, Saint Joseph my father and lord, my guardian angel, intercede for me.

After

I thank you, my God, for the good resolutions, affections, and inspirations that you have communicated to me in this meditation. I ask your help to put them into effect. My immaculate Mother, Saint Joseph my father and lord, my guardian angel, intercede for me.

SPIRITUAL READING

Before

Come, O Holy Spirit, fill the hearts of your faithful and enkindle in them the fire of your love. Send forth your Spirit, and they shall be created. ℟. **And you shall renew the face of the earth.**

Let us pray.

O God, who has taught the hearts of the faithful by the light of the Holy Spirit, grant that by the gift of the same Spirit we may be always truly wise and ever rejoice in his consolation. Through Christ our Lord. ℟. **Amen.**

After

℣. We give you thanks, almighty God, for all your benefits, who live and reign for ever and ever. ℟. **Amen.**

℣. May the Lord grant us his peace. ℟. **And life everlasting.**

BLESSING BEFORE A MEAL

℣. Bless us, O Lord, and these your gifts, which we are about to receive from your bounty, through Christ our Lord. ℞. **Amen.**

(Add for midday)

℣. May the King of everlasting glory make us partakers of the heavenly table. ℞. **Amen.**

(Add for evening)

℣. May the King of everlasting glory lead us to the banquet of life eternal. ℞. **Amen.**

THANKSGIVING AFTER A MEAL

℣. We give you thanks, almighty God, for all your benefits, who live and reign for ever and ever. ℞. **Amen.**

℣. May the souls of the faithful departed, through the mercy of God, rest in peace. ℞. **Amen.**

SOME ASPIRATIONS

A clean heart create for me, O God. (Ps 51:12)

A contrite and humble heart, O God, you will not despise. (Ps 51:17)

A poor and lowly servant am I.

All the glory for God.

For those who love God, all things work together for good. (Rom 8:28)

For you, O God, are my strength. (Ps 43:2)

He must increase, but I must decrease. (Jn 3:30)

Here I am, for you did call me. (1 Sm 3:5)

Holy Mary, our hope, seat of wisdom, pray for us.

Holy Mary, our hope, handmaid of the Lord, pray for us.

Holy Mary, star of the sea, help your children.

I can do all things in him who strengthens me. (Phil 4:13)

I do believe; help my unbelief. (Mk 9:24)

I give you thanks for all your benefits, even the unknown ones.

In you, O Lord, I take refuge: let me never be put to shame. (Ps 31:1)

Lord, increase our faith. (Lk 17:5)

Jesus, Son of David, have mercy on me, a sinner! (Mk 10:47)

Jesus, Jesus, always be Jesus to me.

Lord, you know all things, you know that I love you. (Jn 21:17)

Lord, that I may see. (Lk 18:41)

Lord, what do you want me to do? (Acts 22:10)

Mother of fair love, help your children.

My Lord and my God. (Jn 20:28)

Not as I will, but as you will. (Mt 26:39)

Queen of Apostles, pray for us.

Sacred Heart of Jesus, grant us peace.

Show that you are our mother.

Sweet Heart of Mary, prepare a safe way for us.

PRAYERS FOR THE DEAD[1]

The Church *prays for the dead*, and this prayer says much about the reality of the Church itself. It says that the Church continues to live in the *hope of eternal life*. Prayer for the dead is almost a battle with the reality of death and destruction that weighs down upon the earthly existence of man. This is and remains a particular *revelation of the Resurrection*. In this prayer Christ himself bears witness to the life and immortality to which God calls every human being.[2]

PRAYERS AFTER DEATH

When death has occurred, the following prayers may be said:

Saints of God, come to his/her aid!

Come to meet him/her, angels of the Lord!

℞. **Receive his/her soul and present him/her to God, the Most High.**

May Christ, who called you, take you to himself;
may angels lead you to Abraham's side. ℞.

Give him/her eternal rest, O Lord,
and may your light shine on him/her for ever. ℞.

Let us pray.
All-powerful and merciful God,
we commend to you N., your servant.
In your mercy and love,
blot out the sins he/she has committed
through human weakness.
In this world he/she has died:
let him/her live with you for ever.
We ask this through Christ our Lord.

℞. **Amen.**

---

1. Ben 1988.
2. CTH 25.

These verses may also be used:

℣. Eternal rest grant unto him/her, O Lord.

℟. **And let perpetual light shine upon him/her.**

℣. May he/she rest in peace.

℟. **Amen.**

℣. May his/her soul and the souls of all the faithful departed, through the mercy of God, rest in peace.

℟. **Amen.**

GATHERING IN THE PRESENCE OF THE BODY

When the family first gathers around the body, before or after it is prepared for burial, all or some of the following prayers may be said. It is most fitting that family members take part in preparing the body for burial.

All make the Sign of the Cross:

In the name of the Father, and of the Son, and of the Holy Spirit.

℟. **Amen.**

Then one member of the family reads:

My brothers and sisters, Jesus says: "Come to me, all you who labor and are overburdened, and I will give you rest. Shoulder my yoke and learn from me, for I am gentle and humble of heart, and you will find rest for your souls. Yes, my yoke is easy and my burden light."

The body may then be sprinkled with holy water.

The Lord God lives in his holy temple yet abides in our midst. Since in Baptism N. became God's temple, and the spirit of God lived in him/her, with reverence we bless his/her mortal body.

Then one member of the family may say:

With God there is mercy and fullness of redemption. Let us pray as Jesus taught us:

Our Father...

Then this prayer is said:

Into your hands, O Lord,
we humbly entrust our brother/sister N.
In this life you embraced him/her with your tender love;
deliver him/her now from every evil
and bid him/her enter eternal rest.
The old order has passed away:
welcome him/her, then, into paradise,
where there will be no sorrow, no weeping or pain,
but the fullness of peace and joy
with your Son and the Holy Spirit
for ever and ever.

℞. **Amen.**

All may sign the forehead of the deceased with the Sign of the Cross. One
member of the family says:

Blessed are those who have died in the Lord,
let them rest from their labors,
for their good deeds go with them.

℣. Eternal rest grant unto him/her, O Lord.

℞. **And let perpetual light shine upon him/her.**

℣. May he/she rest in peace.

℞. **Amen.**

℣. May his/her soul and the souls of all the faithful departed, through
the mercy of God, rest in peace.

℞. **Amen.**

All make the Sign of the Cross as one member of the family says:

May the love of God and the peace of the Lord Jesus Christ
bless and console us
and gently wipe every tear from our eyes:
in the name of the Father,
and of the Son, and of the Holy Spirit.

℞. **Amen.**

One of the following prayers may be said:

A. For the family and friends

God of all consolation,
in your unending love and mercy for us
you turn the darkness of death
into the dawn of new life.
Show compassion to your people in their sorrow.
[Be our refuge and our strength
to lift us from the darkness of this grief
to the peace and light of your presence.]
Your Son, our Lord Jesus Christ,
by dying for us, conquered death
by rising again, restored life.
May we then go forward eagerly to meet him,
and after our life on earth
be reunited with our brothers and sisters
where every tear will be wiped away.
We ask this through Christ our Lord. ℟. **Amen.**

B. For the deceased person and for the family and friends

Lord Jesus, our Redeemer,
you willingly gave yourself up to death,
so that all people might be saved
and pass from death into a new life.
Listen to our prayers;
look with love on your people
who mourn and pray for their brother/ sister N.
Lord Jesus, holy and compassionate,
forgive N. his/ her sins.
By dying you opened the gates of life
for those who believe in you:
do not let our brother/ sister be parted from you,
but by your glorious power
give him/ her light, joy, and peace in heaven,
where you live for ever and ever. ℟. **Amen.**

For the solace of those present the minister may conclude these prayers with
a simple blessing or a symbolic gesture, for example, signing the forehead
with the Sign of the Cross. A priest or deacon may sprinkle the body with
holy water.

PRAYERS AT THE GRAVESIDE

Aside from the time of mourning, the month of November, including especially All Saints' Day and All Souls' Day, is a traditional time for visiting graves, as is the anniversary of death. Some or all of the following prayers may be used at the graveside of a family member or friend.

All make the Sign of the Cross. The leader begins:

Praise be to God our Father, who raised Jesus
Christ from the dead. Blessed be God for ever.

All respond:

Blessed be God for ever.

The following Scripture text may be read: 2 Cor 5: 1

We know that if our earthly dwelling, a tent, should be destroyed,
we have a building from God, a dwelling not made with hands,
eternal in heaven.

After a time of silence, all join in prayers of intercession, or in one of the litanies or other prayers. All then join hands for the Lord's Prayer:

Our Father…

Then the leader prays:

Lord God,
whose days are without end
and whose mercies are beyond counting,
keep us mindful
that life is short and the hour of death is unknown.
Let your Spirit guide our days on earth
in the ways of holiness and justice,
that we may serve you
in union with the whole Church,
sure in faith, strong in hope, perfected in love.
And when our earthly journey is ended,
lead us rejoicing into your kingdom,
where you live for ever and ever.

℟. **Amen.**

or:

Lord Jesus Christ,
by your own three days in the tomb,
you hallowed the graves of all who believe in you
and so made the grave a sign of hope
that promises resurrection,
even as it claims our mortal bodies.
Grant that our brother/sister N. may sleep here in peace
until you awaken him/her to glory,
for you are the resurrection and the life.
Then he/she will see you face to face
and in your light will see light
and know the splendor of God,
for you live and reign for ever and ever.

℞. **Amen.**

℣. Eternal rest grant unto them, O Lord,

℞. **And let perpetual light shine upon them.**

℣. May they rest in peace.

℞. **Amen.**

℣. May their souls and the souls of all the faithful departed, through the mercy of God, rest in peace.

℞. **Amen.**

All make the Sign of the Cross as the leader concludes:

May the peace of God,
which is beyond all understanding,
keep our hearts and minds
in the knowledge and love of God
and of his Son, our Lord Jesus Christ.

℞. **Amen.**

ADDITIONAL PRAYERS FOR THE DEAD

℣. Do not remember my sins, O Lord,

℟. **When you come to judge the world by fire.**

℣. Direct my way in your sight, O Lord, my God,

℟. **When you come to judge the world by fire.**

℣. Give him/her eternal rest, O Lord, and may your light shine on him/her for ever,

℟. **When you come to judge the world by fire,**

℣. Lord, have mercy.

℟. **Christ, have mercy; Lord, have mercy.**

All:

Our Father ... trespass against us.

℣. And lead us not into temptation,

℟. **But deliver us from evil.**

℣. From the gates of hell,

℟. **Deliver his/her soul, O Lord.**

℣. May he/she rest in peace.

℟. **Amen.**

℣. Lord, hear my prayer,

℟. **And let my cry come unto you.**

℣. The Lord be with you.

℟. **And with your spirit.**

Let us pray.
Lord, welcome into your presence your son/daughter N.,
whom you have called from this life.
Release him/her from all his/her sins;
bless him/her with eternal light and peace;
raise him/her up to live for ever
with all your saints in the glory of the Resurrection.
We ask this through Christ our Lord.

℟. **Amen.**

For a parent:

Let us pray.
Almighty God,
you command us to honor father and mother.
In your mercy forgive the sins of my/our father/mother
and let me/us one day see him/her again
in the radiance of eternal joy.
We ask this through Christ our Lord.

℟. **Amen.**

For a brother or sister:

Let us pray.
God, our Maker and Redeemer,
in your mercy hear my/our prayer.
Grant forgiveness and peace to my/our brother/sister N.,
who longed for your mercy.
We ask this through Christ our Lord.

℟. **Amen.**

℣. Give him/her eternal rest, O Lord,

℟. **And may your light shine on him/her for ever.**

℣. May he/she rest in peace.

℟. **Amen.**

℣. May his/her soul and the souls of all the faithful departed, through the mercy of God, rest in peace.

℟. **Amen.**

BAPTISM OF A PERSON
IN DANGER OF DEATH

In the case of a person who is at the point of death, that is, whose death in imminent, and time is short, the minister, omitting everything else, pours natural water (even if not blessed) on the head of the sick person, while saying the usual sacramental form.

At the moment of death or when there is urgency because of imminent danger of death, the minister, omitting all other ceremonies, pours water (not necessarily blessed but real and natural water) on the head of the child and pronounces the customary formulary.

If persons who were baptized when in danger of death or at the point of death recover their health, they are to be given a suitable formation, be welcomed at the church in due time, and there receive the other sacraments of initiation. In such cases the guidelines should be applied when sick persons recover after receiving not only baptism but also confirmation and eucharist as viaticum.[1]

RITE OF BAPTISM[2]

In the case of a person who is at the point of death, or in imminent danger of death, the minister, omitting all other ceremonies, pours water (not necessarily blessed, but real and natural water) on the head of the person, while saying:

N., I baptize you in the name of the Father, ✠

The minister pours water the first time.

and of the Son, ✠

The minister pours water the second time.

and of the Holy Spirit. ✠

The minister pours water the third time.

It is desirable that there should be one or two witnesses. If able to do this, an adult candidate is required to make a profession of faith, such as the Apostles' Creed (p.37) before the Baptism.

---

1. *Rite of Christian Initiation of Adults* 371, 374.; *Rite of Baptism for Children* 21..
2. Cf. RCC; *Rite of Baptism for Children* 21.1, 160, 164; *Rite of Christian Initiation of Adults* 373.

INDEX